PRAISE FOR

NOMADS I HAVE KNOWN AND LOVED

"A brilliantly crafted portrayal of these most remarkable tribal peoples. Presented with passion and compassion by one who has become a part of them as they have become a part of her...their beloved Irma 'Aissu'. "
Carol Scribner, author, photographer Winner of the Nautilus Book Award

"With the insightful words and stunning photographic images of Irma Turtle, *Nomads I Have Known and Loved* takes us into the hearts and minds of Africa's indigenous peoples. We learn of customs and cultures that have stood the test of time, steadfastly maintaining their integrity and dignity in the face of modernization. But, more than that, the book affords a fascinating glimpse into the daily lives of these men and women of Africa. We also get to know the book's author--a woman of remarkable character, courage and a heart as big as the African continent itself. In the depth of her interactions with people whose lives she's touched, we can palpably sense the profound love she feels for them, and they for her "
Alan di Perna, journalist and author: Guitar Masters, Intimate Portraits

"Irma Turtle's spellbinding prose and stunning photographs transport your mind and body deep into the souls of these exquisite nomads and their magical lands."
Andrea Markowitz, award winning writer and editor

"More than just a lively account of African tribal life and festivities, "Nomads I Have Known and Loved" is a touching autobiography of a courageous woman. Irma tells us her story with a combination of humor and lyricism that intimately captures the nomads she met, the places where they lived, her personal and spiritual growth, and our hearts. This story is one verse in Irma Turtle's long and magical life tale, maybe a favorite verse and certainly one that has spanned nearly three decades. To those of us who love her and who sing in her chorus line, we can say with certainty that her voice is worth hearing!"
Karen Leeds, Artist

"I was instantly transported deep into a time so alive with life, custom and tradition that the people, proudly performing their ancient rituals of song and dance began to move and interact with each other right before my eyes. I was there... from the moment I held the cover in my hand, to when I closed the book. And the journey continues. The world Irma's photos and words bring to life, that of the African nomad, will embrace me forever."
Raleigh R. Pinskey, international speaker, best selling author of multiple books

FOREWORD

by
Sandra Lorde Michael, Writer, multiple Clio Winner, adventurer

"Who am I and where do I fit?" are questions we Westerners ask anew throughout our lives, but which Africa's nomadic cultures answered hundreds and thousands of years ago. Perhaps few people in modern times have lived with and been loved by these ethereal people more than Irma Turtle. As she brought other adventurers, followed by help in whatever form was needed, to the people and land with which she'd fallen in love, Irma Turtle became Aissu -- Africa's Godmother. The tribal people -- the Tuareg, the Wodaabe, the Hamar, and the Himba -- opened their homes and their hearts in unprecedented ways.

In *Nomads I Have Known and Loved*, Irma allows us to fall in love, too. We come to see ourselves mirrored in kind and ancient eyes. And the questions flow: What is beauty? What does it mean to be resilient? What holds lasting value and enduring meaning? What is home? Thank you, Irma, for taking us with you and walking us deeper into the heart of the Great Mystery that holds us all.

NOMADS

I HAVE KNOWN AND LOVED

A Thirty-Year Journey into the Cultures, Customs, Homes and Hearts of Africa's Tribal Peoples.

IRMA TURTLE

Cover Photograph: Assalama, Tuareg lady from Dagaba,
Air Mountains, Sahara Desert, northern Niger
Irma Turtle

Cover Design: Heinz Kagerer

NOMADS I HAVE KNOWN AND LOVED, A Thirty-Year Journey into The Cultures, Customs, Homes and Hearts of Africa's Tribal Peoples.

ISBN- 978-0-9907838-0-0

Printed in the United States of America

A VERY SPECIAL DEDICATION
TO MAYA MOLTZER , my very dear soul sister and travel companion, I cannot think of Africa without thinking of you!

Video film maker par excellence, you toiled endlessly at filming the TurtleWill story, providing us with miles of wonderful and unique footage of all TurtleWill's various programs. You did double duty in the Volunteer Medical Clinics. You funded so many projects from life-saving healthcare to wells, schools, co-ops and animal herd reconstitution. And you were always there to give me emotional support when I needed it.

Maya and Rhodette at our tiny oasis at Dubla, northen Niger, Sahara Desert, 2008.

Together we have spent so many hours in Africa, both working, and playing. My memories include, most of all, the special times we would take after the programs ended and the others had all gone home, to relax by ourselves at our "private oasis" at Dubla, out in the middle of nowhere, no more than three palm trees on a hillock of sand pretending to be a dune in an otherwise flat desert.

It became even more wonderful when we added little Rhodette to our crew, the sweet little puppy who we rescued out in the desert. How hard I cried when we had to turn her over to Alhousseini for safe installation with his family when it was time to go home.

Thank you for all our precious time together.

With love always, Aissu

5

DEDICATION TO CAROL BECKWITH AND ANGELA FISHER

**To my dear friends
Carol and Angela,**

You two are among the people I most admire in the world. Given that the other three with whom you share the top of my list are Zena, Warrior Princess; Sheena, Queen of the Jungle; and Angelina Jolie, you can see how I pick my heroines...by their abilities to change the world...fictitious or not.

I am forever grateful to you because, first through your books and then through our friendships, you opened the door to Africa for me, and took me by the hand and led me in.   What a gift!

I will always cherish you deeply.

Irma, Aissu

*Carol Beckwith, Irma Turtle, Angela Fisher
1997 Cave Creek, Arizona*

*We are each modeling my new line of TurtleWear "bush clothing" designed to raise money for Africa and made from African fabrics.
Carol's dress was called "Carol's Choice" and Angela's was called "Angela's Fancy."*

TABLE OF CONTENTS

ACKNOWLEDGEMENTS

My book, *NOMADS I HAVE KNOWN AND LOVED*, pays homage in text and photos to only a few tribal groups: the nomadic Tuareg of the Algerian, Nigerian and Malian Sahara, the nomadic Wodaabe of Niger, the nomadic Himba of northern Namibia and the Hamar of southern Ethiopia. However, it is also dedicated to all those tribal peoples I have known and spent time with during the course of my 28 years traveling, first through my adventure travel company, Turtle Tours, and then through my humanitarian foundation, TurtleWill. I offer all these tribes my thanks and gratitude for all that I have learned from them.

Together with them I have led a life of such extraordinary experiences, as if I were constantly living inside a National Geographic documentary. From these peoples I have learned to speak with my eyes and my smile when no translator was present. There is so much truth in that old adage, "the eyes are windows to the soul."

There is perhaps nothing more important than the recognition of our common humanity; that just remembering someone's name each time you see her or him fills that person with such pleasure and trust; that reaching out to give an ailing person a simple touch on the cheek, the shoulder or the hand can make them feel so much better, without words or medicines. And, of course, the most important thing you can bring with you, anywhere, is love.

I have learned that a diversity of cultures makes us much richer as a sentient species on Planet Earth, that we have much to learn from each other in sharing our uniqueness in beliefs, traditions and rituals. Most illuminating is the discovery that we all share the same goals...to see ourselves and our children evolve into thoughtful conscious beings with a respect for each other, for ourselves and for the planet.

This book is also dedicated to all those wonderful travelers and volunteers who have been with me, so many of you on multiple trips; who shared in the same experiences of awe and gratitude at the kindness, generosity and fortitude of all the various tribes we visited; at how we were welcomed time after time into homes, huts and tents without hesitation, even when we were unknown visitors; and how we so openly shared our traditions, stories and songs with each other. There are so many of you to thank, the list would go well into the hundreds. I hold each of you very dearly in my heart. Thank you too for making my life possible and I offer you all my love and gratitude.

Irma Turtle   "Aissu"

INTRODUCTION

WHY THIS BOOK IS AN HONOR AND AN OBLIGATION TO WRITE!

It was January, 1992 and I was trekking in the Congo Basin in the heart of Central Africa with a group of 12 clients, two guides and more than double our number of porters. We were in search of the Baka Pygmies. As we moved noisily along the trail we were overtaken by a Pygmy family of three: father, mother and child. They walked quietly and swiftly, and nodded at us shyly with diffident, gentle smiles when we opened our ranks to let them pass. They were moving their home. They were naked except for a few leaves. All they carried with them were a basket and a machete each, while the woman carefully cradled in her hands a big ember of fire wrapped in a banana leaf. That was it. These Pygmies were moving in 1992 exactly as they had been moving for thousands of years, carrying with them little more than this ceremonial ritual fire which was never allowed to go out.

This was for me one of those many overpowering moments of wonder that I have had the privilege to experience in the bush. Moments of admiration for cultures that still manage to survive in the simplest and purest of ways. Moments of awe at their unselfconscious persistence. Among these tribal groups some are nomadic and others are sedentary. What's so remarkable about them, what makes them stand out in a world fraught with change, with confused identities and with struggles for survival at the barest minimum, is that they have lived for centuries true to their cultures and their traditions...and with almost no concessions to the modern world. This is not an easy feat.

Irma with Matka, wife of Wodaabe Chief Tambari Girka, Maradi region, Niger.

These tribes are among the world's few remaining primal societies, still governed by ancient codes of behavior and traditions, where material possessions are little more than the few essentials required for dress, eating and sleeping; in which individual roles are clearly defined for men and women; where everyone from the youngest to the oldest participates and where everyone counts. They share a positive sense of belonging, a comfort and security in being part of a group.

Such a primal society gives them a "freedom" that we have long forgotten in our contemporary, modernized, westernized world. I speak of a freedom from role searching, goal seeking, values discerning, from all those modern neuroses that seem to be part of the malaise of the 20th and 21st centuries. They have the confidence to just be who they are, and who that is they don't have to question. Their cultures and traditions are so deeply ingrained that no reminders or explanations are needed. Theirs is an un-self-conscious existence in the middle of a modern world. They stand out as isolated fortresses of tradition, doing things their own way, with pride in their heritage, with a fierce sense of belonging, while the rest of the world barrels right on by them, frenetically, chaotically, directionless, identity-less.

In 1985, I set off on my own self-conscious search when I left a major career in advertising, one that began on Madison Avenue and culminated with my being director of a branch office in Brazil for the international firm Ogilvy & Mather for three years. At age 40, I quit. I felt I had paid my dues doing what was supposedly expected of me by society at large, and it seemed time to find out who I really was, what was really important in life and just what I truly wanted.

Travel, especially in the more remote and exotic places of the world, has always attracted me, and tribal peoples, primitive societies and art has always been my great loves. Starting an adventure travel company specializing in remote tribal peoples was the niche I quite quickly found for myself. My years in advertising dealing with a multitude of personalities and staff had taught me well how to manage such a multi-faceted operation. I could get the job done and keep everyone happy and reassured at the same time, from tribal friends to clients.

I found myself quickly welcomed into tribal families, comfortably hobnobbing with local chiefs, delightedly holding babies named after me, and happier than I had ever been in my life. And it was a fair trade. I was always a welcome guest bringing with me on each of my visits to my tribal friends the supplies they needed...like coffee, salt, tea, sugar, cloth and medicines as well as other interested travelers who, like me, felt honored and privileged to be among them. The niche was just right. It didn't take me long to exchange the persona of "white collar business woman" for "tribal godmother."

My personal odyssey with these tribes, during the years of travel, of getting to know them, of living with them, of loving them, gave me insights into my own life. As I understood the simplicity of their lives, I got down to the essence of mine. Am I closer to the real me, "an ancient nomad from way back?" Yes. I am not suggesting that a life of rote adherence to the dictates of a given culture is admirable or enviable, nor that it would work today for most of us. We are too "socio-psychologically" evolved. But these cultures do serve as a reminder to those of us caught up on those ever quickening treadmills of the 21st century, that life need not be so complicated, that many of the burdens of achievement and materialism we weigh ourselves down with are unnecessary, that the values we have placed on our devotional altars may not be the wisest choices, and that often personal happiness can be as simple as the right to roam the world's open spaces, or to follow your herds.

My three Hamar tribe goddaughters from Ethiopia:
Irma Rachel, Irma Sarah and Irma Leah and I.

But how have these tribal groups managed to preserve their cultures in such a crystalline way? What exactly is their secret in sustaining themselves over the centuries? You might assume it has to do with an isolation and lack of exposure to the outside world. But the outside world has always been there at their doorsteps.

So, what is it? After years among them of observing, pondering and wondering, I came up with the answer that works for me.   I call it

"The Abraham Syndrome"

Having grown up surrounded by the ancient traditions and rituals of Judaism, the more I traveled I couldn't help but be aware of the variety of rituals built into all these other cultures I was getting to know. Rituals are the physical and symbolic expression of a culture or tradition, and their enactment is as strong a statement of adherence to that culture as any. The more I looked, it seemed quite clear that rituals were the glue that held these groups together.

Tuareg family, Elekat, Azouas region northern Niger photo by Melissa Cole.

....Ritual decoration plays an especially important role. It's the most difficult to deny or erase. As I see it, this all goes back to the days of Abraham and his covenant with God. "You will be my chosen people and I will give you the land of Canaan." God said. "You only need do one thing for me... circumcise your boys on the eighth day of their birth." A brilliant maneuver in which he set the Jews indelibly and undeniably apart from the rest of the population. If you were a male, there was just no denying it, and if you were a female, you certainly knew the requirements. And...as a member of the tribe, whichever sex, you had to honor the ritual or not be accepted. Pariah status has never been popular in any crowd.

Therein lies the genius of ritual decoration, which includes body scarification, tattooing, mutilation, hairstyles, jewelry and clothing.

These elements set your group apart from every other group. In any given marketplace where various tribes congregate, you can immediately recognize who is your friend and who is your enemy. When survival is a concern, it helps you gather quickly together in self-preservation. And when there is no outside threat, these ritualistic elements still make assimilation into the more dominant group difficult because body tattooing, scarification and mutilation just aren't that easy to erase. Unique ceremonies and rites of passage also set you apart but they are not indelible in the way that physical body ritual is.

Wodaabe Beauty Queen, Azouas region, northern Niger.

Combining physical body rituals with identity is certainly one way to hold a culture together. There are too many ingrained barriers, superstitions and taboos to break down. I like to think of this as "The Abraham Syndrome."

Take the very beautiful Wodaabe women of Niger. There is just no chance for confusion as to who they are. And note, they have almost never married outside their group. It starts with their facial scarification...elegant tattoo-like geometric designs around the corners of the mouth and eyes that mark the lineage and the tribe.

And then there's the hairstyle, not to be found anywhere else. A bun of hair piled forward at the forehead, a braid above each ear, and a braid in the back. Their very distinctive costume includes several large hoop earrings in each ear, all the red and yellow beads along with brass and leather amulets they can find, and blouses and skirts of indigo blue cloth, embroidered richly in a variety of colors and symbolic geometric designs.

13

Wodaabe men are not so colorful until it's Gerewol festival time, when the male beauty and charm competitions take place. But once these men have put on all their make up, painted their faces with different colors and designs, donned their elaborate costumes and begin their festival ritual, there's not another group of men in the world who can compete with their special look. Believe me, you would never confuse a Wodaabe for anyone else.

The Tuareg culture also has its uniqueness. A Tuareg adult male will never be parted from his turban or sword which he dons as a symbol of adulthood. Although men from other cultures in West Africa's Sahara and Sahel regions also use the turban as protection from sand and dust, they do not cover their faces as part of their religious or cultural creed. The Tuareg culture is the only one in Islam where the men go veiled but the women don't. The women can also be readily identified by their hairstyles which include a series of tight long braids wrapped in different patterns unknown to any other culture. They also cover themselves with silver amulets. The Tuareg are also known for their unusual festivals which include ceremonial dress for men, women, donkeys and camels as well as camel races, dances and singing.

Rituals like these work towards preserving the integrity and homogeneity of the tribe, because if you don't participate, you are an unacceptable member of your society. There is no room for renegades. This is the "Abraham Syndrome" as I see it: rituals contributing aggressively to the continuity of a group through their ability to keep the group culturally intact despite all possible incursions from the modern world. Once this barrier breaks down, total assimilation into the larger dominant group is much more predictable. The Tuareg and the Wodaabe are like many others still similarly intact, who have hung on to who they are.

My book, ***Nomads I have Known and Loved***, is a personal testimony through both photos and text to the tenacious and steadfast survival of these tribal peoples into the 21st century. I share with you what I have learned in my travels in Africa, introducing you to some of the many tribal peoples who became my dear friends and companions, have influenced my life and with whom I have spent some of my most precious moments. I invite you to enjoy with me their traditions and rituals as I came to know them.

I promise you a celebration of the diversity of humanity, and an admiration for their uncompromising ability to be who they are. These people, as individuals and as groups, have helped me find the essentials of my own life. For this I will be forever grateful. The following pages, text and photographs, are meant to illustrate the ways in which through ritual decoration and ceremony they have remained true to their origins and their hearts.

Tuareg woman and her donkey in ceremonial regalia. She is wearing the traditional dress of the Air mountains, as is her donkey who is covered in traditionally decorated cushions and rolled blankets, making her a very comfortable seat.

Tuareg male in traditional indiigo blue clothing, Air Mountains, Niger.

CHAPTER ONE

THE BIRTH OF TURTLE TOURS

"For the first time in my life I truly feel like I have found my roots."

With tears in my eyes I had just made this staggeringly important, heart-baring comment to my companion."
"That's nice," he responded rather dismissively.
"No, no, you don't really understand. I really feel I've found my home."
"That's nice." he said again, making an effort to produce a little more enthusiasm.

"You still don't really understand." I said. "My people were wandering around here 4,000 years ago too!"

"What do you mean, 'YOUR PEOPLE'? What do you mean, 'HERE?'." Driss said.

"I'm Jewish."
"No you're not. You're American."
"I'm Jewish and American." I said more emphatically.
"No, you cannot be Jewish. You are American."

My insistence was a bit shocking to him. The Sahara Desert, after all, was the ancient domain of his people, the Tuareg, and no female American upstart was going to claim any dominion.

This discussion could have gone on for a while except my companion Driss ended it abruptly by asking me the most important question in his mind, "what religion are you?" For many Muslims in his part of the world all Jews were Israelis. There was no understanding that Jews lived in other parts of the world as well. So from his perspective the conversation was closed because he knew I carried an American passport. Presumably, if I were American I must be Christian, just as all people in Algeria, Tuareg and otherwise, are Muslim.

Driss, seated beside me on the small sandstone rock outcrop, was dressed in the garb of his people. He wore a big black turban which completely enveloped his head and all of his face right up to the very bridge of his nose, revealing only his beautiful almond shaped brown eyes. His traditional big baggy flowing pants called "sarrouel" had a crotch so wide and deep that it fell almost to his knees. These were desert-adapted pants allowing for easy movement when leaping up onto a camel. They were tight at the ankles so they wouldn't ride up and they were decorated with simple white embroidered designs down the sides. His shirt was a loose and comfortable tunic covering his arms to his wrists and reaching almost to his knees. Everything he wore was black with the exception of his handmade sandals which were crafted out of red and green dyed leathers.

Tuareg man from the oasis of Timia participating in the Spear Dance.
Air Mountains, northern Niger.

Driss

was a Tuareg from southern Algeria and we were in the middle of the vast Sahara desert, all of which was his home. Driss was the local guide appointed to travel with our small band of French tourists and me, the only American, on a 10-day overland trip across Southern Algeria from west to east, culminating with a climb up onto the Ajjers plateau on the border with Libya to see 6-8,000 year old rock paintings.

The conversation for me was not over, however, although it quickly became a private internal one. I did indeed feel for the first time in my life like I had actually found my roots. I felt at home. Imagine! I had quit a major international career in advertising with Ogilvy & Mather in July, 1984 because I wanted something more meaningful in my life. And I had known about this very beautiful rock art for 17 years but didn't think it was accessible.

Now it was January, 1985 and I was putting the two dreams together! Here I was deep in the Sahara Desert. The fact was, I had little idea of what to expect from the Sahara, the world's largest desert. I'd been to the Negev, and I'd been to the American West. I knew I liked deserts. So chances were, I'd like the Sahara.

I was in no way prepared for the magnitude of my reactions. Upon arrival at the tiny airstrip at Tamanrasset in southern Algeria with the French tourists I had joined, we were greeted by a group of veiled and turbaned men who were to be our drivers and guides. These were the legendary Tuareg, the "blue men of the Sahara." those warrior, caravan-running, camel riding nomads of ancient stock and legendary fame. They were about as mysterious and elegant as men can get, in long flowing robes and turbans revealing no more than their dark almond shaped eyes. This was fantasy come to life.

The next day we began our 10-day journey in our little caravan of three 4WD Toyotas, driving from west to east across southern Algeria, through the Central Sahara. The first two days were just okay...we were traveling through the volcanic and craggy Hoggar mountains in the southwestern corner of Algeria. They repelled me with their severity and harshness... jagged mountains and stony landscapes everywhere under foot. I found them hostile, aggressive. Absolutely not my favorite type of scenery.

In theory I loved deserts but after two days out I was seriously wondering just what I had gotten myself into with this Sahara Desert thing. I had all the wrong equipment, froze my tush off at night in a less than winter weight sleeping bag until one of the Tuareg staff lent me a blanket, and I had to break my toothbrush out of the ice in my little metal cup each morning. What's more, my electric razor filled with sand and broke, and there was almost no water to wash my hair. I was cold and dirty. This was less than pleasant.

During the day under the hot heartwarming desert sun I promptly forgot the night time ordeals. I was absolutely mesmerized by our drivers. From the very first I felt a comfort and a security among these men who, even though they specifically had chosen to replace their camels with Toyotas, were obviously the masters of this desert domain. There was a self-assuredness and self-reliance about them, a dignified hospitality and courtesy that was almost kingly.

By day three everything was different. We were deep in the Tassili du Hoggar, one of the Sahara's most highly acclaimed beautiful regions. I was sitting with Driss on the above mentioned rock in a section called the Tagrera and my heart cracked open wide.

The scenery had drastically and suddenly changed. Surrounding me in a 360° vista was the most extraordinary vast and sacred landscape I had ever seen in my life...a remarkable region of endless panoramas, where the horizon stretches forever, where the ground beneath you is all smooth sand and everywhere there are wonderful huge rock shapes jutting up out of it.

Sahara desert, southern Algeria, Tagrera region.

It's as if a great master architect had taken a can of shaving cream, colored it beige and sprayed out a whole floorful. And then to add to this glorious vastness that seemed to extend without end, the great master had another creative idea. Into this soft, unevenly wavy base, he took chunks of eroded sandstone rock of different sizes and shapes and with them he whittled wonderful formations... playful magical sculptures, a big one like a dinosaur here, a little one like a mushroom there, a bunch of elephants way over there.

He placed them at random in different spots and they sank gently into the sand while the wind sculpted out hollows around them. We stood at the top of the hollows and slid down on our bottoms to the base of the sculpture below.

And then there were the undulating dunes...some tall, some small, some medium. All different sizes were everywhere, gentle waves of sand here, higher crests there as if frozen in mid-action. Variations of color were almost subliminal depending upon the age of the sand and the sunlight to make them more or less golden.

Camping in Tagrera, Tassili du Hoggar region, southern Algeria
Note the tiny person in the foreground!

This was a landscape that was so breathtakingly beautiful with its extraordinary combinations of sand and rock everywhere, so pristine and primordial that I knew I had found what had been missing all my life. I was home at last. And all this was only magnified by the remarkable affinity I felt with the very people who were guiding us, the Tuareg, the ancient nomads of the Sahara.

Who could have imagined I would go almost overnight from International Advertising Exec to "Queen of the Sahara?"

I left my advertising job at Ogilvy & Mather in July, 1984 because I was looking for something to do that would really help the world and make my heart sing. In the meanwhile, because I knew that my own personal aria might take a while to discover and perfect, I hung out my shingle as a marketing consultant. In November I was interviewed by a trade magazine where I met the director of a business school in Paris. He insisted there was no one in France with my particular skill in business direct marketing and offered to introduce me to companies at an industry convention in Paris in January, 1985.

Rock painting, polychrome cattle, 6000 BC Jabbaren, Ajjers Plateau, south eastern Algeria.

A week before I was to leave for this convention in Paris there was an article in the New York Times travel section about the 8,000 year old rock art on a mountain plateau referred to as the Tassili du Ajjers in southeastern Algeria. I had always wanted to see this amazing, hauntingly beautiful rock art. I had tried 12 years before in 1972 to book a trip there. At the time the cost was $1,300 and I was making only $8,000 a year running an art book club for

Harcourt Brace in Boston. I assiduously saved my money for 10 months, and then called to book the trip. I was told that the Tuareg nomads in the region would rob you and maybe even kill you. The price had gone up and it wasn't due to inflation.

So, when I saw this new notice 12 years later about a French company offering to take you to the very same Tassili du Ajjers and with no caveats that you might not return alive, I was ecstatic. I quickly booked myself on the trip before I left for Paris and applied for an Algerian visa. The booking was quick but the visa part sure wasn't. For some unrevealed reason my visa request had to be sent to Algiers by telex for final approval. I was on tenterhooks until the very last moment, receiving the visa only on the morning of departure.

I spent four days at the convention in Paris and landed Citroen, the automobile company, as my client. Then I flew down to the desert with the French group. It was a 10 day trip with the rock art, the supposed "piece de resistance" of the voyage waiting patiently, as it had already done for millennia, to be ogled, admired and photographed on day seven. But by day three, having reached the Tassili du Hoggar, I was already madly in love with the desert itself.

I staggered through those days lost in an aesthetic fog. Never had I seen anything so beautiful. It was the vastness, the beauty, the pristineness, the majesty, the creativity of rock formations, the marriage of beige sand and grey rock, the sacredness of this part of the Sahara desert that caught me and locked me in its embrace.

The rock art up on the Ajjers Plateau was our last stop. Yes indeed, the paintings were extremely beautiful, tiny soft colored paintings on deeply patinated sandstone cave walls. They had that kind of magnificence and simplicity that defies size. If you saw them first as reproductions in a book they would give you the impression that they were monumental, full wall size. In reality they were minoscule, but still beautifully evocative, gentle, reminiscent of the purity of Matisse cutouts.

But...they didn't evoke anything close to the emotional pitch I had experienced in the region of sand and dunes of the Tassili du Hoggar. To put it succinctly, my ancient Jewish soul had finally found its roots in the holiness of the desert and reclaimed the tenderness and softness of my mother in the great undulating femininity of its dunes. And, thus, Turtle Tours, my new adventure travel company, was birthed like magic.

After that tour I flew back up to Paris, made arrangements with a French adventure travel company to explore more, then headed back down into Algeria to spend another three weeks exploring other corners of the Algerian Sahara in order to develop itineraries I thought would appeal to my future American clientele. I returned home to New York in April, 1985 and registered my new business, Turtle Tours.

What started out as a simple adventure to the Sahara Desert to see the rock paintings in southeastern Algeria turned out to be the greatest, longest and most important adventure of my life.

Rock carving known as the "Crying Cow," c.8,000 B.C southern Algeria, outside Djanet.

This was the beginning of 28 years of travel, exploration, profoundly moving human encounters and deeply satisfying humanitarian work. My territory covered the Sahara desert as well as all over Africa and other parts of the world where I could and would get to know and love unique and exotic tribal peoples and nomads, all of whom would more than fill me with joy and love and admiration.

When I began Turtle Tours I was really lucky! I drew nothing but the best of travelers with whom to share these journeys. They were totally flexible, relaxed and easy to be with. If there were a flat tire they patiently bided their time along the side of the road talking to each other or photographing plants. If we were late for a meal because we had an especially long and wonderful visit with a particular tribal group, nobody got cranky or grouchy. And if we had to make camp in the dark because we were having too good a time out on the road with the tribal peoples somewhere and arrived late at the campsite, everybody lent a hand so that camp was set up as fast as possible.

My travelers were exemplary and compassionate travelers and always treated the tribal peoples with dignity. They asked first if they could take photos and eagerly participated in our conversations with elders and chiefs about traditions and customs. When emergency funds were needed to send a sick tribal person to the hospital they all chipped in. And they were hungry for information. At night over dinner we would discuss what we had seen that day as well as what we would encounter the next day.

I was making an impact on the lives of these dedicated travelers in introducing them to cultures so unique and different. And I was also doing a service to the tribal peoples by introducing them to outsiders who treated them with respect and dignity, and who were very interested in meeting them and exchanging ideas. We always brought gifts when visiting, the same way we do at home. My travelers were in no way the "snap the photo and run" type. The Turtle Tours motto was "Tourism should be reciprocal, not exploitative."

"My" American tourists were quickly deemed the best nationality to travel with by the local tour operators. I often received compliments from local staff and tribal peoples on the niceness of the Americans who traveled with me. They would complain about the French who always criticized the food. And they would complain about the Italians who would force the drivers to drive all day, right up until sunset to make sure they didn't miss a thing. The Italians were the crazy daredevils, always taking risks in the Sahara "sandwhacking" their way without Tuareg guides across uncharted terrain, and then getting lost or having to be helicoptered out. But my Americans were perfect, easy-going, amiable, willing to put up with almost anything. And, they gave very big tips! With Turtle Tours the end of every trip was like Christmas for the staff.

This all made me feel really blessed. I was doing the work I loved in sharing the special parts of Africa and its people with my clients and my clients were all wonderful people. For the first 12 years of Turtle Tours I didn't have a single difficult traveler. I guess the law of averages was starting to kick in because for the next five years I did usually have one or two cranky types on each trip. A lesson in humility for me perhaps! Then TurtleWill started and my world changed once again.

.

Teheydeymount, Tuareg from Ikanan's camp, Air Mountains, Niger.

Haidera, a beautiful young woman from the Tuareg community of Teshaq, outside of Timbuktu, Mali.

In Memoriam
Haidera died in childbirth in 2005 because she was too weak to ride the camel to the hospital in town, five miles away.

CHAPTER TWO

WHERE THE MEN GO VEILED AND THE WOMEN DON'T

Tuareg man from Timia wearing many amulets around his neck. Each one contains a specific prayer written on a piece of paper, such as "May my family always be healthy." These prayers are purchased on demand from the marabouts or holy men. They are then taken to the leather workers who will cover them in these leather casings.
Air Mountains, Niger.

One of the first Tuareg people I got to know was Ahmed, my driver/guide. Ahmed was the son of Boubeker, an intrepid Tuareg considered the foremost Saharan guide of all and responsible for opening up a good part of it to tourism. He went in together with a French explorer named Frison-Roche and charted areas that no-one had gone into before, except maybe a misplaced nomad or two, who certainly would have exited at the first opportunity. Nomads move with a purpose. They have herds and families to water and they can't carry it with them. So their migrations take them only where they are sure to find it. Tourists and explorers wander more at random. As long as they have 4WD and enough water they can cart along with them, they can visit all those areas that nomads would never have dared. And so he did. His son Ahmed was one of the top of the line Saharan guides.

1985 was the official launch of Turtle Tours and I started with a flourish and three clients. Our destination naturally was the Sahara Desert, specifically that very same central Sahara of southern Algeria where I had found my roots the first time. My clients were Monique, a very wonderful French friend I had made on that first exploratory trip into the Sahara the year before, and Ray and Nancy, who were sent to me by the Algerian embassy in Washington. We met first in Paris at a pre-trip meeting to get acquainted. Monique has one of those laughs that make you think of a handful of cascading rose petals after they have been thrown up into the air, and Ray and Nancy have a zest for travel and life that made everything bode about as well as it could. There was instant chemistry among this group of ours.

We flew down to Algeria and landed at the "Tam" (short for Tamanrasset) airport, which was filled with its usual host of milling Tuareg men in long blue caftans, turbaned and veiled up to their eyeballs. It couldn't have been more exotic. Here we were, once again, among the mysterious "Blue Men of the Sahara"…as exciting as something out of "Tales of 1,001 Nights." Pinching oneself would not have been an unusual reaction.

Sahara Desert, Tagrera, Tassili du Hoggar region southern Algeria.
The Toyota is always the vehicle of choice!

The next morning our little expedition headed out in our single land cruiser, the vehicle of choice in this part of the world, for our 12-day expedition into the Central Sahara, with Ahmed at the helm, and Mohamed, our Tuareg foot guide, coming along to keep us on the safe and narrow. Our hearts were all pounding. There we were about to penetrate the vast expanses of the Sahara, heading off into the unknown, no roads, no markers, no gas stations, hopefully with all the necessary food and water, and guided by these great looking veiled men. Even after years of travel in the Sahara I have never ceased to have this feeling of wonderment and anticipation.

Ahmed, our driver/guide, had the dignified serious demeanor of the noble Tuareg, and in his no-nonsense, "this is my job" attitude there was something about him that was certainly reassuring. Mohamed was much warmer, a crinkly smile showing in his eyes, which was all that was showing at the time. With him we knew we'd have a good time. With Ahmed, we knew we would make the trip and live to tell about it, both of which options we were indeed counting on. Both men were dressed in black and topped with turbans. Ahmed's was black and wrapped traditionally. Mohammed's was white and wrapped with much less ceremony,

Mohamed at rest in typical Tuareg pose. Sahara desert, southern Algeria.

more like a headband with his crinkly hair hanging out. Both men wore long flowing black tunics and the traditional sarrouel, the very baggy pants that make camel riding easy and comfortable.

The Tuareg have been fierce warriors and masters of this domain for centuries. Tall and pencil thin, with their heads swathed in 15 feet long turbans, covering everything but their eyes from the neck up, and long indigo blue or black robes covering all from the neck down, they are indeed imposing. The indigo blue is the fabric of choice among the Tuareg. It is very regal, very expensive and the color wears off on the face and hands, tinting the skin blue. For this reason, the French army, upon first encountering Tuareg warriors in the Sahara and not knowing who they were, labeled them "the Blue Men."

A full 15 feet are required as the turban or "tagelmoost" doubles as a death shroud in case they should die out in the desert, away from the home tent. The Tuareg are the only group in Islam where the men go veiled and the women don't. The veil, covering the face up to the bridge of the nose, makes these men about as mysterious as one can get. And given that the original Tuareg, of which Ahmed is one, are ancient descendants of the early Caucasian Berbers, they have the most extraordinary almond shaped brown eyes. Self-respecting Tuaregs still think it shockingly indecent for a man to let his face be seen by anyone to whom he owes even the least formal respect, so the eyes are usually all you ever get to see.

The women are equally handsome, regal, and most independent. They dress primarily in flowing indigo or black shawls and black wrapper skirts, and wear whatever silver jewelry they own, mostly pendants, some of which is bound into their black braids. As this is one of the world's very few matrilineal cultures, a male Tuareg child will be a noble if his mother is of noble descent. Accordingly, his most important male relative is not his father but his maternal uncle. When a woman marries, she retains full title to all her personal property including livestock. Women, as guardians of the Tuareg traditions and laws, are responsible for passing on the knowledge of Tifinah, the written language. Tifinah is one of the three written languages in all of Africa and is of Berber origin. The other two are Ethiopian, the first an ancient religious script Guezz and the second, a contemporary script.

Tuareg men court their women, recite poetry and race their camels. Theirs is a code of chivalry long forgotten. For the longest time, when people couldn't quite figure out who the Tuareg really were, they were thought to be descendants of a lost group of crusaders. Their swords and camel saddles marked oddly enough by a prominent cross, certainly pointed that way. The final word seems to be out now on the subject. The original Tuareg are descendants of a splinter group of Berbers who fled south in the 7th and 8th centuries from the northern regions of the Algerian Atlas fleeing religious persecution, when Islam was on its big conversion campaign.

The name "Tuareg," meaning "the abandoned," was given to them by the Arabs who considered them infidels in their early attempts to convert them to Islam. They call themselves "Imohagh," "to be free." They fled first into the most inhospitable areas of southern Algeria: the rugged and craggy mountains of the Hoggar and the mountains of the Ajjers. Nobody could get to them there, and they hung out in their goat skin tents coming down only to lead their own salt caravans across the desert and to raid and pillage others.

For centuries the nomadic Tuareg made their living as caravaneers with salt being the main commodity; as brigands, raiding others or being paid not to; and from the garden rent they received from their vassal clients. Today brigandry is over, but they are still caravaneers and the salt trade continues to flourish. Their animal of choice continues to be the camel. Sheep and goats fill out the herd. Ladies ride the donkeys.

So there we were with our two veiled and turbaned Tuareg, heading out into the depths of the Sahara, a small party of intrepid explorers. We too were all veiled and turbaned by

Tuareg male in traditional Indigo cloth. New indigo cloth has a shiny metallic sheen. The cloth here has been well washed!

this point, but not to look mysterious. Water is at a premium in this part of the world and we just hoped to keep out some of the sand and dust inherent to any Sahara crossing.

The Sahara may be hot, the Sahara may feel dry, but the Sahara is never boring. The Sahara, contrary to public opinion, is only one seventh sand. The rest, approximately 3,000 miles wide and 1,000 miles deep, is rock. Rock of all sorts, in all shapes and forms, conventional and otherwise, and depending on where you are, mixed in with no sand, a little sand, or a whole lot of sand. There are craggy volcanic mountains; table mesas called "hammadas," lumpy huge accumulations of sandstone that form canyons, spires and castles, all a function of what the wind's been up to; flat gravel plains called "regs," pressed so flat that it looks like a steam roller went over them. There are the immense undulating dune fields called ergs; dried up ancient river beds that actually do run with water when a flash flood comes down from the mountains; neolithic rock art dotted all over the place; ancient acacia and tamarisk trees for a bit of shade; flowers that will spring forth everywhere in just a few days after a rain has come; gazelles, foxes, jackals, gerbils, scarab beetles; criss-crossings of men and camels in caravans carrying salt and grain; and nomad camps scattered here and there.

The here and there depends on the where of the water. There is indeed water under most of the Sahara, the problem is how to get to it. Where it is easy to reach, there are lots of nomads, even full blown oases lined with palm trees. Where it is too deep or the bedrock too hard to get through…forget it. The only people you will see in areas like this are tourists, carrying all their necessary water with them.

Our first few days were wonderful. Remarkable landscapes that you never could have imagined. Our route took us first through the craggy volcanic Hoggar mountains, to my mind about as hostile and unfriendly a place as you can find. Nancy, Ray and Monique were fascinated, but then, I like the soft sensual touches of the dunes, the ongoing waves of sand that make the place much more feminine than masculine, welcoming rather than aggressive. Ahmed, his face always veiled, maintained his reserve, but Mohamed was loosening up, dropping his veil, and joining more and more in our sense of comraderie.

From the hostile Hoggar we moved due south into what is for me the paradise of the Sahara…the Tassili du Hoggar, that region of undulating sand and rockscapes where I finally met my roots and where my spirit comes to rest. We wandered in awe. In the mornings we headed out on foot with Mohamed, while Ahmed went ahead with the vehicle. Like a true Tuareg, Mohamed's stride across the desert exemplified the typical grace of his people, who all have an unparalleled erect and dignified posture and a walk that is more of a glide than a stepping motion. We glided each morning for about 3-4 hours…easy walking with plenty of time to stop and gape at all around us. Then we would meet up with Ahmed and the vehicle for lunch and hike again in the afternoon.

Evenings around the campfire would begin with rituals of Tuareg tea and Mohamed's Tuareg bread. This was no simple tea service as we know it. Tea for the Tuareg is both functional and ceremonial. Tea may be all a Tuareg has for breakfast, but it is always the very first act of hospitality when a guest arrives. The Tuareg traditionally drink three glasses,

Heading into the craggy volcanic Hoggar Mountains, southwest corner of Algeria.

Ray, Nancy and Monique on a "glide" with Mohamed.

each one sweeter than the last. According to tradition, the first glass is bitter like death, the second is sweet like life, and the third, sugary like love. You must drink all three if you are invited to tea. There's even a fourth very weak one for children. The tea of choice is Chinese green tea, which is super strong and must first be boiled and rinsed, all of which takes place with a great deal of ceremony in the tiniest tea pot you can imagine. But as the tea is so strong, the servings are tiny as well, poured usually into a small collection of decorated shot glasses. The artistry of the tea maker is judged not only by the quality of his brew, but by his ability to pour it from on high, creating a thick foam or head on top of the liquid tea. He starts pouring from his tiny pot about 2 feet above the tiny glasses. The objective of course is to keep the tea inside the glasses while creating the foam at the same time. Mohamed is expert at making foam. Monique and I usually arrived in time for the third glass. Just as well because the first two glasses are generally too strong for my herbalized tastes. Too much tea and I would never get to sleep.

Mohammed taught us a simple Tuareg poem which captured the essence of the tea ceremony:

> "Now, let's stop work, until tomorrow,
> Light the fire,
> Call the guests,
> We're going to make tea."

Tuareg bread, which Mohamed made regularly, is quite special, if only for the process. It is actually baked in the sand under hot coals. This is one of the original unleavened breads, made of flour, water and a pinch of salt. It's made into a big ball, punched around a bit in the pan and then flattened out into an inch high pizza shape. Meanwhile, a hot fire has been burning in the sand. Once the firewood has been reduced to coals, they are all swept clear, a flat circular depression is dug in the clean sand underneath the fire, the raw dough is placed directly on the sand, and is then covered up with more clean sand. Finally the coals are put back on top. The bread then cooks in this sand oven for about 30 minutes. When it is ready, it is dug out, dusted off with a knife or washed off with water. The result is a thick crusted, rather heavy but tasty bread called "gallette" somewhat reminiscent of the taste and texture of a New York bagel. It is eaten plain or as a delicious version called "tagellah" where it is broken up into bits in spaghetti or stews dripping with camel butter.

Ahmed to me typifies the noble Tuareg of Algeria, extremely proud of their culture and very blue. As descendant of the original "Blue Men," he wore a turban and clothing of indigo blue. Day by day he became more blue. Ahmed looked like he fell into a ream of carbon paper. Mohamed, a not noble Tuareg with traces of Negroid blood, dressed daily in a white turban and a black caftan, known as a "boubou," in local lingo. Mohamed was not blue. To me he represented more the jolliness and gaiety of black Africa, which certainly was in his genes, while still maintaining the chivalric code of the Tuareg. When he was out with us on our treks, he cavorted and played like the rest of us. We were very glad he came along. Smiling, friendly and open, he offered a different insight into the same culture.

Mohamed playing hide and seek on a sandstone formation in the desert during one of our daily "glidings."

Bela family, former slaves of the Tuareg in Mali.

The nomadic Tuareg are quite an interesting group of people with a complex socio-political structure. Not only are there noble Tuareg clans, there are vassal clans, slave clans and blacksmith/silversmith clans. It all came about quite "logically." As nobles, the men and women weren't allowed to do any physical labor. The camels and herds still needed to be watered, and the grain needed to be ground. The solution? Take slaves, for one. Which they did, primarily by raiding Arab and Black Africa. There were also some other sedentary groups in the neighboring areas and further south who had no problem with this supposed menial labor. Hey, for a buck, they would do anything. And for their labors, they also got protected from other raiding groups. Hence, vassal clans. In Algeria these groups are called Harratan. In Mali they are the Bela and in Niger they are the Bouzou.

Treated very well by their masters and bosses, these groups long ago adopted the same Tuareg way of dress. So now they all look alike. The only dead giveaways are usually in the skin color and facial features. A noble Tuareg is generally very light-skinned compared to his slave and vassal buddies, what with his Caucasian Berber ancestry. As the slaves and vassals came partly from Arab groups but mostly from Black African groups, their features usually reflect their Negroid origins. As there was also a lot of intermarrying, or at the very least siring of children, there was also a lot of mixed blood. But, if you can't figure out who a guy or girl is by looking, you can always ask them their clan name. That tells all.

Slavery actually only ended officially in this part of the world in the 60's. In defense of the system though, slavery here was never on a par with slavery in the US. The Tuareg have been Muslim since about the 11th century and the dictates of Islam require that you treat your slaves like family. So they did.

As for the separate class of blacksmiths, these are the revered but "untouchables" of the Tuareg world. I am not sure what it is about fire, but it seems that blacksmiths from early cultures all over the world have always generated fear and live as a caste apart. Among the Tuareg, their women are the leather workers. Tuareg from these clans never marry outside their group. But they figure very importantly in the culture as they are responsible for the only ornamentation the Tuareg traditionally use. The blacksmith/silversmiths make all the silver amulets, pendants, crosses, rings, swords, spears and daggers with which the Tuareg love to adorn themselves. Their women make the beautifully and intricately ornamented leather saddle bags, storage bags, pillows and tent ornaments that decorate a Tuareg's home and his camels. So, they really are quite indispensable. Kind of a catch 22...you can't love them but you can't do without them. Otherwise, you surely would be a poorly dressed and unornamented Tuareg.

The final group in this complex social-political structure are the "marabouts" or holy men. They reside over the fabric of the faith, Islamic and otherwise, and are the producers of the lucky amulets and leather charms that all Tuareg men and women wear for protection.

After 12 days with Ahmed and Mohamed we finished our Sahara journey and returned to "Tam" safely. We parted rather formally from Ahmed and thanked him for a job well done. We felt very satisfied. His driving and his skill at finding the most glorious campsites each

Tuareg men from the Air Mountains, Niger.
Note the different style of turban which changes from region to region.
Hanging around the neck of the man on the right is his traditional Tuareg leather wallet
which holds important papers, like his Identity Card, money and pipe.

night were impeccable. Ahmed and I worked together on subsequent trips and he always provided the same excellent quality of service.

   With Mohamed it was different. Like a true Tuareg, he had guided us on foot over trackless domain for days. He had an unerring sense of where he was going, and we never felt him falter. And like a true Tuareg he treated us with the courtesy due visitors. The difference was that in letting down his veil he had equally let down his guard and allowed friendships to foster. From Mohamed we parted fast friends. We had shared equally in our love of where we were and this gave us a bond that would never break.

Tuareg woman from Timia, Air Mountains, northern Niger.

Tuareg woman, Air Mountains, Niger.

Tuareg mothers and babies from the Air Mountains, Niger.

43

Traditional braided hairdo of Tuareg women.

Traditional embroidered blouse of Tuareg women of the Air Mountains, Niger.

Traditional Tuareg head cloth of indigo, still retaining its metallic sheen.

CHAPTER THREE

LEARNING TO "YOUYOU," THE ART OF ULULATION

The following year, 1986, I was back in the Algerian Sahara with another small group of Turtle Tours clients. We had been traveling overland through the desert, this time heading east from "Tam," through the Tassili du Hoggar. We were carrying our own full water cans because there was almost no water on our route, or at least little that was reachable, so, on the eighth day, when we reached the well at Tadent, we were all very pleased at the prospect of bathing, and quite happily helped our Tuareg drivers draw water from the well.

The well was located in a flat scrubby area near a dry river bed. The surrounding bush was dense so it was easy to slip out of sight and do a little personal bathing. While we were there three Tuareg ladies, whose camp was apparently just down the dry river bed, came by on foot for water as well. They were each dressed in traditional white overblouses with black embroidery, black wrapper skirts and silver amulets and jewelry. I helped them draw their water and fill their "guerbas," the traditional goat skin water bag carried by Tuareg on the sides of their camels or hanging or strapped to the underbelly of their donkeys. They stopped to admire all my travel amulets which are a combination of silver pieces from all over the world that I always wear on my trips. They have all been given to me by a diversity of people who love me so they can easily protect the whole group traveling with me, and, equally important, they never fail to be a great conversation opener with tribal women everywhere. Then, we sat down in the sand to "chat" as best we could.

I grabbed from our truck the West African "kora," a guitar-like instrument I had just purchased in "Tam," and asked them if they could play it. They shook their heads. The Tuareg possess only one stringed instrument, the "hamzad." There are very few women remaining who know how to play it and it is very rare to see. My kora was a much bigger instrument with a host of strings and didn't resemble their hamzad in the least.

Next, I sat down on the sand in my own comfortable sarrouel and put myself in the proper clapping position for a "Tinde," sang a few Tuareg syllables as best I could and indicated that I thought it would be a great idea to have a "Tinde" right there. And, believe it or not, I made an inspired attempt at a "youyou." The haunting "youyou," the ululating call of the Tuareg women, will always be one of my sharpest memories. It is a primordial cry, used to punctuate both celebration and lament, and whenever I hear it it runs right up and down my spine, evoking goosebumps all over my body. It is emitted by women from many cultures found in Africa, Asia and the Middle East.

My attempt was probably much more like a turkey gobble but they quite easily got my point and sat down to join me. For about five minutes we had a great impromptu "Tinde," using the backside of my guitar as the drum, with the three women singing and ululating and me clapping. Then, much to my disappointment, they stood up, picked up their water bags and walked away. Just like that. The party was over. Quite dejectedly I watched them slowly disappear down the river bed. So I got up too and began to help make camp.

*Tuareg woman playing the Hamzad, which is the only stringed instrument the
Tuareg possess. Only a few old women are left who can play it.
She is fully dressed in traditional Indigo dyed cloth. She is also using the
dye from her cloth as a cosmetic and has carefully rubbed it into the skin on
her nose and mouth as well as her hands.*

That evening we had dinner by the campfire and everyone headed off to sleep. But just as I was getting into my sleeping bag I heard music...singing and drumming...coming from further down the riverbed where the Tuareg supposedly had their camp. Salah, my Tuareg guide, walked over to me and said, "Irma, those women are singing and drumming for you. They want you to go down there and join them." Wow! How wonderful!!! I looked around to see if any of my group wanted to go with me, but they were asleep, so off I went with Salah to find the women. A five minute walk and we were there.

There were about 20 women (with not a man in sight), all seated in a tight circle on the ground, all in black shawls draped over their heads. Smack In the middle of them was a Tinde drum. Some of the ladies had babies asleep in their laps and a few larger children were clustered on the edge of the group playing quietly. There was no fire, only a lot of starlight. One of the ladies I had met in the afternoon quickly grabbed my hand and pulled me down into their group so that I was seated right in the middle of them.

With only the stars for light, all I could see were their draped black silhouettes, the whites of their eyes and their teeth, and their glowing white "houmensa" amulets around their necks, made of the traditional five pieces of shiny abalone shell representing the hand of Fatima, the sister of Mohamed. Surrounding us in the background I could barely make out the outlines of several leather skinned traditional Tuareg tents with tiny fires glowing. The women began to sing and two women did the drumming on the Tinde while this etched itself deeply into my memory.

Tinde drum assembled.

Occasionally one or two women would syncopate with the most glorious "youyous" I have ever heard. As it was apparent I wanted to learn this, the two ladies on either side of me took charge and took turns showing me how. One of these was a very beautiful but toothless old crone who was absolutely intent that I learn that very night. She would grab me by the arm, pull me towards her and emit the shrillest possible "youyou" directly into my ear so that my entire head, not just my eardrum, reverberated with the sound. Then she would look at me, smile encouragingly and wait while I attempted to imitate her. Despite the horrific sound that I was making, they all loved it when I tried to "youyou," and there wasn't a woman or child in the group who didn't keep encouraging me. I stayed there with them until midnight, the singing, drumming and "youyou"ing continuing relentlessly.

It took me another two years to master a decent "youyou," one that actually raised eyebrows. Who would ever expect that such a sound could come from the mouth of a "toubab" or white person. And I have only my Tuareg lady friends at Tadent Well to thank, and a night in the Sahara among the Tuareg that I will never forget.

Tuareg granny, Timbuktu region, Mali.

The drum, or "Tinde," is made from a large mortar and pestle that women use all over Africa to grind grain. The mortar bowl is covered tightly with a goat skin that is kept wet to maintain the tension. The rope that binds the goat skin over the bowl is then bound equally tightly around two large pestles that are secured on opposite sides of the drum to ensure the tautness of the skin, kind of like a tourniquet. In sandy areas young girls sit on either end of the pestles, like a see-saw, to give even more tension. In rocky areas small boulders are used instead. The "Tinde" ceremony takes its name from the drum that is used. Sometimes this Tinde drum is accompanied by an even more unusual drum, created by using a flip flop sandal to beat on a small upside down calabash bowl bobbing in a larger calabash of water. It has a wonderful resonance. And finally, of course, there are the empty 20 liter plastic jerry cans for water or gasoline which also serve double duty as impromptu drums!

Photos on both pages show traditional ornaments and clothing including hair braiding styles, silver amulets, silver and beaded necklaces, fully decorated festival blouses sewn locally with embroidery and spangles and facial decorations made of silver foil and dyed leather.

Generations of Tuaregs, Sahara Desert, Mali and Niger.

Tuareg chief and his extended family.

53

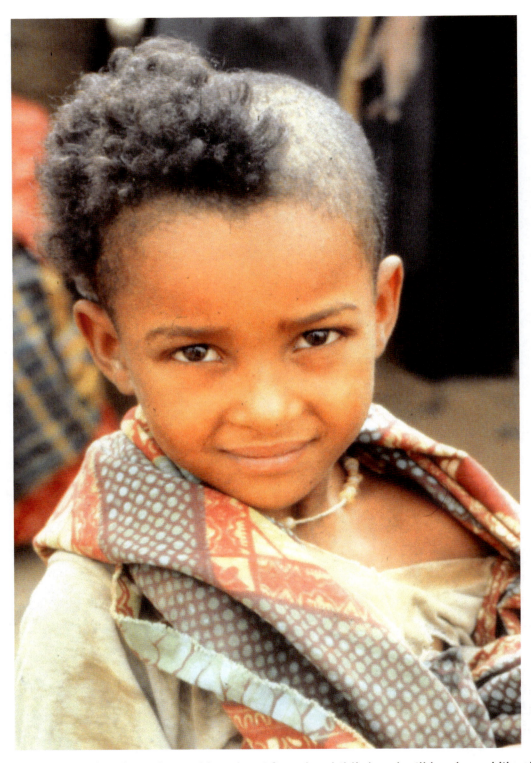

Young Tuareg girl with traditional hairdo. Often the child's head will be shaved like this. The reason for leaving the tuft of hair is that, should it be the child's time to die, God must have a bit of hair tuft with which to gently reach down and pull the child up into heaven. northern Niger.

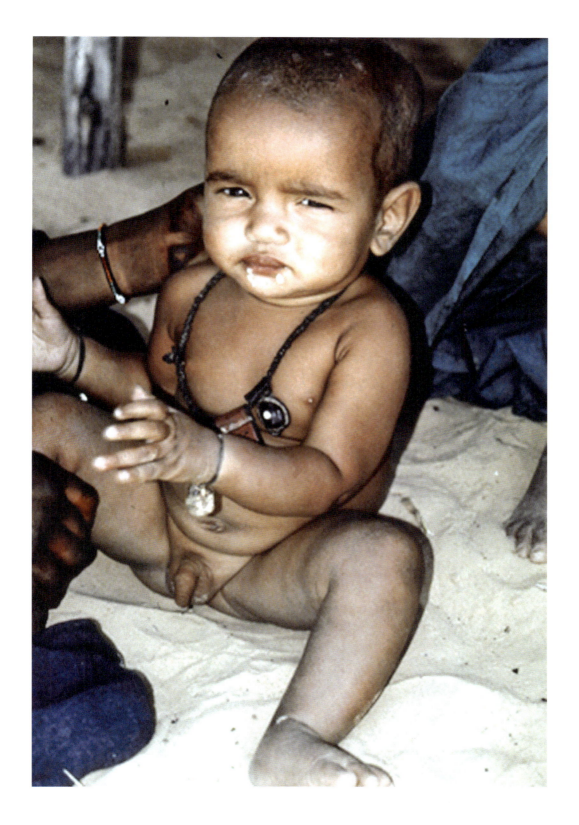

Little Tuareg baby boy from Assana community. He is wearing the traditional protective amulets that all Tuareg children and adults wear.
Timbuktu region, northern Mali.

Everyone is alert as visitors arrive. The young girl is wearing traditional Tuareg braids in her hair and a very faded indigo blue caftan.
This traditional Tuareg family tent is made out of reed mats. The bed inside is a very simple design with "spools" at the corners and thin slats of a soft, lightweight wood. Woven mats are then layered on top of the slats and spool to make a softer bed. Several people may sleep on it.
Such constructions are easy to dismantle and be mounted on donkeys whenever the family needs to move to a new area for richer pasturage for their herds, and of course, for water. Sahara Desert, northern Niger.

Tuareg women waiting their turns to draw water from the local well while watching the ongoing activity taking place. Sahara Desert, northern Niger.

Tahasimin and her baby Yazmin, Girka Well community, Maradi region, northern Niger.

Tuareg men in the oasis town of Timia sharing some tobacco for their pipes
Air Mountains, northern Niger.

CHAPTER FOUR

THE GERIATRIC LUNATIC EXPRESS

My next major expedition into the world of the Tuareg and the Sahara took place a year later in 1987. I'd been warned that this trip would be a tough one. 1,562 miles of travel starting from Tamanrasset, Algeria in the heart of the central Sahara, overland in a southwesterly direction across Mali to Ouagadougou, Burkina Faso, is no piece of cake, especially when it's to be done in 16 days. And we would be camping out in the open, like on all my other trips, and eating around the campfire.

I had dubbed the group I was leading "the Geriatric Lunatic Express". Departure date was set for late February for our special African Overland Expedition. George, my oldest client on this trip, was 78, followed by Edwin a 72 year old retired postal worker, and two highly artistic ladies: Mary, a sculptress of 64 and married to George, and Rita, an actress/producer of 63. These four were followed by my old friend Devin, age 42, and Cecile, a cute young French girl of 26 whom I had inherited in Paris just before departure, as assistant cook to Bruno, the French guide accompanying our trip. A group to open your eyes...or to keep your eyes open.

Dunes in the Sahara, northern Niger.

Our first few days of encountering the Sahara desert were sublime. Beautiful, sensual, curvaceous dunes undulating into immense seas of sand. Sandstone canyons creating walk-in sculptures. Surreal volcanic chimneys of basalt in the Hoggar Mountains silhouetted by spectacular sunsets. Camps at night cradled in the hollow of a dune with millions of stars overhead. My gang romped and cavorted in this vast playground. With cocktails at six, duck a l'orange (from a can) at seven and beddy-bye by 9 so you can fall asleep counting the shooting stars, what more could you want. The Sahara was indeed as wonderful as I had promised. Even the camping was easy. Set up your cot, lay down your sleeping bag, brush your teeth, a few dabs with water and off you go. You never feel dirty because the Sahara is so dry.

It was on the fourth day when it began to get tough. We had just finished crossing the Tanezrouft desert, one of the most deadly portions of the Sahara, in the southwest corner of Algeria. Almost no wells and no landmarks. This is the kind of terrain where those rare blind Tuareg guides mentioned in old Saharan history books would have a heyday. The only way to figure out where you are is by smelling the sand. So dangerous is this portion of the desert that the Algerian government requires you to take a special guide with you from Tamanrasset. Cuts down on their having to send rescue planes to find you, hopefully before you have withered away into a dried old piece of leather, like some of the corpses of donkeys and camels we saw en route. These animals had made it to the wells. But they couldn't reach the water.

We made it through without any problems and without a blind guide. The tough time started with the Algerian border passport control that we had to pass through, before crossing into Mali. We first arrived at the barren, recently constructed border town of Timiaouine at 2PM and were informed by the one, less than cordial official I could find, that it was siesta time, and customs wouldn't open until 4PM. Quite perfunctorily, he directed me and my group to wait outside. "Wait where?" I wondered. There wasn't one bit of shade in this whole godforsaken town, that looked more like the world after nuclear fallout than anything else. Just a few mud brick buildings the color of the surrounding sand. That was it. The only option was to install everyone in the street against the outer wall of the customs building, in the wee bit of shade that it created.

This was hardly an acceptable situation. A bunch of senior citizens, pressed up against a wall in 110 degree heat, is not a pretty sight. So, back into the barracks I went. Sure enough, there was one more soldier in there, stretched out languidly on one of the few beds. Noticing me peeking around, he wasted no time with the more customary introductions of civilized folk. "Hello," he said, and got right to the point. Would I like to go to bed with him?

Well, this certainly presented a challenge. Under more ordinary circumstances, which would probably refer to absolutely any other time, place or man, my normal response would have been somewhere between incredulity and anger, but circumstances here were different and I needed his help far more than he needed mine. So my feminist nature quickly acquiesced to my more wily feminine nature. Now was the time to flatter my opponent, not distance him.

"What a lovely offer," I said in French, butter melting in my mouth. "What could possibly be more appealing than to have an intimate moment right here and now, in the middle of the desert, in this raging heat, with an unknown soldier, but I am afraid my duty weighs far too heavily for me to indulge myself in such a luxury." His eyes lit up with anticipation then slowly dimmed with disappointment. I continued, "I have with me a group of mental patients, schizophrenic, geriatric lunatics to be precise, whom I have taken from the hospital, for a vacation in the Sahara. But the heat and travails of the journey have been too much for them. They are all now very sick and I must get them to the hospital in Gao as soon as possible. I am afraid that some of them may die. Won't you please find a way to speed us on our journey without making them wait in the heat until 4PM for our exit visas?"

I had him right where I wanted him. Disappointment turned into sympathy and then fear, and he quickly became an accomplice in my cause. The last thing he needed was a bunch of American corpses against the wall of the barracks. Nothing like the threat of losing his job, due to an international incident over a few visas, to get the ball rolling. It seemed most expedient to help us out. I rushed outside and quickly told everyone to act as sick as they could. I wasn't asking too much. The group was looking half expired already.

Going through customs in Algeria is not as easy as in many other countries. You have to declare all the foreign currency you have with you going in, and declare it all once again when you leave. The government wants to make sure you don't change any money on the black market. If you have, you could be in deep trouble. This leaves employees on the lower levels, like custom officials, seriously hoping that you have broken the rules, so that they can catch you at it. As they are usually very underpaid by the government, the bribes you will be willing to pay them to get yourself off the hook, go a long way towards feeding their families. So, they try to make darn sure they find something that is worth a bribe. No such luck with our group. We were all on the up and up. Half dead from the heat, but we had played the game by the rules.

One hour and a half later we were finally out of there. Even I was drooping from the heat. Air conditioning had not yet hit this tiny, bleak outpost in the middle of the Sahara. By the time we were permitted to leave, everyone was more than happy to see us go, especially those thwarted customs officials who waved us goodbye with all the good riddance they could muster. We were exhausted, cranky and just wanting to get the heck out of there. Algeria, goodbye! With luck, Mali would bring us more gentle moments.

But, just as were were making a fast retreat to the edge of town, we were stopped dead in our tracks by what could have been a scene from Tales of 1,001 Nights. At least 50 Tuareg men in full ceremonial dress, all mounted on equally dressed camels, were advancing regally, two by two, towards the center of town. These men were truly splendid as they paraded past in their best indigo blue turbans, veils and long flowing robes. Fantastic! A real "iloughane," the ceremony I had wanted to see for years. Now was no longer the time to leave town. Within two minutes we were back in the center, mesmerized by this unrelenting display of proud Tuareg princes and their astonishingly graceful, gliding mounts.

The parade seemed endless. Pair after pair kept riding by, forming a large circle in the center of town. These were Tuareg of the Iforas Plateau in eastern Mali, many of whom had been repatriated up here due to the ravages of the drought in the early 80's. There are seven major confederations of Tuareg in the world, which include the Ahaggar Tuareg and the Ajjers Tuareg of Algeria, the Iforas Tuareg and the Delta Tuareg of Mali; the Air Tuareg of Niger, and two smaller confederations in northern Nigeria. They all speak "tamachak" and their written language is "tifinah," a derivative of the ancient Berber language. Culturally, they are a very cohesive group. This particular group of Iforas Tuareg, of noble origin, were about as elegant as they could be. Even the camels were superb. Each man was mounted on his best riding camel, of preference a tall, white one.

The Tuareg camel saddle is a decorative accoutrement in itself. It is actually a chair, whose base is strapped directly on top of the hump of the camel. There is a back portion to lean against, and in the front, a tall, narrow pommel, about 2 feet high, which ends in a cross design. These saddles are made of wood, elegantly covered in leather and beautifully ornamented with brass overlays, red and green leather decorations, black designs on the deep red leather seat and often, a bunch of brass bell-like objects to jangle as one rides. The rider sits straight-backed, high up in his chair on the hump of the camel. To accelerate, he uses his feet, which rest barefoot in the crook of the camel's neck. He urges the camel on with soft rapid jabbing motions of his heels into the camel's neck. To steer, he uses the guide rope that is attached to the camel through a ring in his nose. A pull to the left, a pull to the right, and the camel knows just what to do. No bridle is used.

Camel riders arriving in Kogo for a visit, Niger Air Mountains.

In addition to the saddle, the camel is also outfitted in richly decorated saddle blankets, a brass bowl for his water, and several other tasseled ornaments in colored wools and leathers that hang down at his sides. Ritual decoration runs rampant in this part of the world. All these men and all these camels were definitely dressed in their Sunday best.

These Tuareg were all coming into town to participate in an "Iloughane" or "camel dance" ceremony, done in celebration of something special, or just for the fun of it when everyone is in the mood to dress up and show off. When we feel like celebrating, we get dressed up and go out to dinner. Here everyone gets dressed up and goes out for a camel ride, an Iloughane and accompanying Tinde.

Meanwhile, in the center of the large circle of men and camels, seated on the ground in a tiny tight circle of their own, was a group of about eight Tuareg women performing a "Tinde." They were singing, clapping and ululating to the beat of the drums that two of them were playing.

Tuareg Iloughane camel ceremony, Timiaouine, southwestern Algeria.
Note the women seated on the ground behind the dancing camels.

These Tuareg ladies were dressed in their best, and, in true Tuareg fashion, were looking especially blue. They were dressed in deep indigo gauzy shawls, worn almost like saris, draped loosely over their bodies and over their heads. They had obviously spent some time rubbing the blue dye into the skin of their faces and hands. These were indeed the "blue women of the Sahara". Around their necks were hung a number of different Tuareg silver crosses and pendants, including the very special "houmensa" pendant, made out of diamond-shaped pieces of abalone shell, and representing the hand of Fatima, the Prophet Mohamed's sister. They obviously had raided their jewelry boxes for the occasion. Their song was shrill, haunting, repetitive. It was led by one woman, with the chorus sung

Kogo Tuareg dressed in the traditional turban of his clan. His camel is also dressed to the hilt with embroidered saddle blankets and bags.

by all of them. She seemed to be telling a story, and making it up as she went along. It was accompanied by a relentless drumming and clapping. One or two women would occasionally punctuate with "youyous," that piercing, ululating call typical of North African women. If you've seen the film "Lawrence of Arabia," and heard the call the women made when they were urging their men on into battle, you know what I'm talking about. It's a call that will always send shivers up my spine.

   In fact this whole ceremony was sending shivers up my spine. It was primal and it was relentless. It was the "real thing," totally unselfconscious and nobody cared one whit that we were there. As the women's song began to pick up, the men began to parade around them, two by two, in a large circle. If you looked carefully, you could see that all the camels were marching to the beat of the same drummer. Tuareg camels are actually trained to trot to the beat of the "Tinde." All these camels trotting in unison to the sound of this unique, penetrating tribal music was something to behold. Although a camel doesn't look inordinately graceful, when it gets going faster it becomes more and more elegant. When it runs, it sways from side to side, due to the fact that both legs on one side work at one time, rather than front right/back left, like a dog or horse. This gives it a remarkably rolling gait, hence the appellation, the "ship of the desert."

Tuareg men racing with the head shawl of the female singer, northern Niger.

   The men began to ride faster and faster, getting closer and closer to the circle of women on the ground with each turn. As more and more men and camels arrived, some would stand in a line on the side waiting their turn. Once one group finished its circling, it would retreat to the sidelines and let the next team take over. This team would then ride in, tightening their circle each time around the women, who never stopped singing and never looked at the men. So close did the men on camels get to the women that occasionally one of the ladies would have to move the hand that she had been leaning back on, in order not to have it stepped on by a circling camel. Finally, one of the men in the circling team reached down and grabbed the head shawl of one of the ladies and galloped off with it. The other men took off after him on their camels. But nobody was able to catch him. Quite triumphantly he brought the head shawl back himself to the lady. He was the hero of the day.

Tuareg women enjoying a festival, Teshaq community, Timbuktu region, Mali.

   As for my gang, I have never seen a group of people recover from acute heat prostration so quickly in my life. Gone instantly were all the crankiness and killer fatigue we had been feeling. Now, with a remarkable who-knows-where it-came-from agility, they were each climbing onto the hoods and roofs of our trucks to get better views, and of course, photos. Not bad for a group of "geriatric lunatics" who, five minutes prior, looked to be on the verge of extinction due to the hot Algerian Sahara sun. Happily, the customs officers were as mesmerized as we were by the Tuareg performance and no one paid any attention to this amazing, instantaneous transformation of these "very old Americans peoples" into spry young 30 year olds.

   The crowd began to disperse and so did we.   We quickly turned around once again and headed out of town. Our heads full of visions of sugar plum fairies, resplendent Tuareg and racing camels, our sojourn in Algeria among the Blue Men of the Sahara was over.

CHAPTER FIVE

ON MEETING MY SAHARAN COUSINS

I continued my trips into the Algerian Sahara and the sense of having found my roots never left me. Three years later in 1988 I made my first trip into the Sahara of Niger and was greeted by Mano Dayak, the owner of Temet Voyages whom I had contracted to take us through the Sahara. Mano, a handsome and impressive Tuareg of noble origin, was educated in the U.S. and Europe, and was a prominent figure in Nigerian politics fighting for the well-being of the Tuareg community. Mano and I hit it off right away, that very same affinity that I had felt among the Tuareg of Algeria surfacing very quickly. Mano was curious to know just how it was that an American woman had become such a Sahara buff. "I'm Jewish," I offered, to my mind the most direct explanation. "Well, of course!" said Mano. "The Jews and the Tuareg are cousins." Mano didn't go into detail and I presumed he was just flattering me, recognizing in each of our populations the strong fight for survival and speaking more of a spiritual bond than a genealogical one.

But, in 1991 I was in Timbuktu, Mali with a group of Turtle Tours travelers. Timbuktu, so much a part of the Sahara that the desert sands overflow into the streets, is a Tuareg stronghold, and our guide was another very elegant and educated Tuareg named Mohamed Ali. The affinity was similar, and on discovering that I was Jewish, Mohamed Ali promptly announced that the Tuareg and the Jews are cousins. It didn't seem possible that the two men, countries apart, would both be feeding me this same line, so this time I requested an explanation.

The story that he had learned from his father and passed down from generation to generation, was that many hundreds of years ago there was a Jew in Yemen with two sons. The sons decided to emigrate. One headed to Palestine and the other continued westwards and settled in the region of Mali/Niger. There he joined up with the Tuareg but kept his religion, as did his descendants. Today there are still groups of Tuareg in Mali who consider their origins Jewish, among them the Dusahak ("Sons of Issac") near Menaka, and the Imaksharan near Tinderma.

I no longer wondered why I felt like an ancient Saharan nomad from way back. It was quite clear that I am.

*Tuareg woman with unusual head shawl, using traditional West African cloth.
Air Mountains, northern Niger.*

CHAPTER SIX

THE MICROWAVE AND THE FAX

In 1988 another Tuareg friend from Niger, Rhissa Ag Boula, who was working for Mano Dayak as manager of Temet Tours, came to visit me in Carefree, Arizona as part of a promotional business trip. Oddly enough, the Sonoran desert where I live looks quite a bit like Niger. They are both very lush deserts with lots of green and occasional large accumulations of rocks. Unlike Niger though, we have cactus here, the most notable being the huge saguaro, which stands many feet high and often has long arms coming off it. ("Saguaro" means "sentinel" and was so named by the Conquistadores, who early on in the game mistook its nighttime shadowy appearance for forebodingly tall guards, protecting the Indian settlements they were trying to attack.)

Rhissa flew into Phoenix and I picked him up at the airport. We began heading north past the urban sprawl of the city, into the desert. Rhissa was looking more and more perplexed as this was his first experience in America and he had started his journey in the city of San Francisco. Somehow this was not what he was expecting. San Francisco, yes. The Sonoran desert, no. Arizona was looking very much like Niger to him.

We reached Carefree and my house, and he looked around some more. "Irma," he announced, "the only difference between Carefree and Timia," a tiny charming Tuareg oasis in the heart of the Air Mountains in Niger, "is that you have the microwave and the fax."

Of course, there are other differences. We don't use pulley wells with the water drawn up by donkeys or camels to water us and our gardens. Our water flows miraculously in our houses out of taps in the sink. Nor, in fact, do we generally sustain ourselves from what we grow in our gardens. We find our harvest already shrink wrapped in the supermarket. Like those ubiquitous balls of iceberg lettuce. And what we park in our garages as our normal mode of transportation is a four wheeled vehicle, not the four-legged camel. But Rhissa's perception was all that mattered and I wasn't about to disagree with him. Rhissa may have been sophisticated enough to run an agency, use the fax machine and travel to Europe and America, but he was a nomad at heart whose land is the basis for his freedom. Rhissa was concentrating on the essentials and the accoutrements of the modern world didn't fit into the equation.

A few months later Rhissa and I were together again, this time in the north of Niger, at the Tuareg oasis of InGall, waiting for the Wodaabe nomadic festivals to begin. Rhissa was sitting with a group of Tuareg cronies, telling them about his visit to America and to Arizona. I couldn't help but overhear him tell them first about the cowboys he had met, the stagecoach he had ridden in and the gun fight in the street he saw, (I had taken him to visit Rawhide, a replica of an Old West town), and then about my desert home. "And," he said with special emphasis, "there are these trees that look like men." For a brief second I had no idea what he was talking about. But then, of course I knew, the saguaro! Rhissa's perception as soon to be Tuareg rebel chief, was no different centuries later than that of the earlier conquering conquistadores. This put him right up there with the winning teams. Not that he would have ever doubted that. Rhissa comes from a long line of pure noble Tuaregs. With a history and a pride like that to sustain him, he would have no need to worry. How fitting is the old Tuareg proverb, "Let your slaves guard your herds. Let your sword guard your honor."

In 1992 in a conversation with Mohamed Ali in Timbuktu, one of my travelers asked him what was the most important thing in his life. He responded very quickly and simply: his liberty. A poignant answer from a man who was educated at the University of Cairo, runs most of the tourism in Timbuktu and yet still lives far out in a nomad camp with his family.

Here are some more Tuareg proverbs shared with me by my then cameleer friend in Timbuktu, Jiddou Ag Al Moustapha:

It is better to go to sleep angry than regretful.
He who doesn't ask questions, will not know very much.
He who doesn't keep his larder stocked, how will he feed strangers when they arrive?
Milk is nourishment, water is life.
An old man lying down will see something a young man, even stopping to look, won't see.
He who eats well, thinks well.
He who travels much, sees much.

Tuareg men watering their camels at Tagarme, one of the many wells dug by TurtleWill in Niger and Mali.   Air Mountains, northern Niger.

Saharan Wide Diameter Bush Wells

Most wells in the Sahara and the Sahel of Niger are dug by hand. They can be from 40-200 ft deep and take months to finish through the final cementing.

Tuareg women watering their goats and donkeys at Dubla Well, northern Niger

Tuareg boy using his donkeys to pull water from a very deep well while his herd of goats waits patiently to drink. nnorthern Niger.

Tuareg man and his son water their herd of goats at the well, northern Niger.

Tuareg woman hauling water from Issakanane well for her camels and donkeys. Note the pulley system which facilitates her lifting the heavy bag of water. Donkeys are often attached to the ropes to do the hauling, as in the previous photo pg 72, northern Niger.

CHAPTER SEVEN

TUAREG FESTIVAL PHOTOS

Most festivals begin with a parade. It starts at a distance from the festival site, making a grand entrance as it marches in to where the guests are assembled.

Well equipped and outfitted Tuareg donkey rider. Agadez region, northern Niger.

First come pairs of beautifully adorned women riding their equally adorned and outfitted donkeys. Men and camels are also adorned to the hilt. They follow the women on their camels in pairs, all prancing to the same beat.

Tuareg woman from Dagaba dressed and made up for the festival, Agadez region, northern Niger.

Once the parade arrives at its destination, the women descend from their mounts to join in the Tinde or observe from the sidelines. The men who will participate in the Iloughene camel dance or races stay mounted while the others descend to observe as well. These festivals serve as the traditional way to celebrate a good rainy season, births and marriages.

Joining in the parade are men and boys on camels, women and girls on donkeys.

Leather goods, like the beautifully decorated saddlebags slung over the sides of the donkeys, are used both for festivals and for comfort in the tents. Work in leather is generally restricted to certain clans and is only done by the wives of the blacksmiths.

Tuareg women performing a Tinde. Note the rocks which are placed on top of the pestles to tighten the goat skin. Water is also sprinkled on the goat skin for greater tension.

The big bowl sitting on the ground to the right is a second "drum." The half calabash floating upside down in the water is beaten with a flip-flop rubber sandal which makes a wonderfully deep and resonant sound. Air Mountains, northern Niger.

Another Tinde in action. Air Mountains, Niger.

Tuareg men performing the Iloughene Camel Dance around the seated women who are performing the Tinde Ceremony. Kogo region, Air Mountains, northern Niger.

Young Tuareg boys practicing training their camels to prance to the beat of the Tinde drum. Kogo region, Air Mountains, northern Niger.

as

Tuareg women of Teshaq community performing the Tinde. Timbuktu region, northern Mali.

Tegbus dance which can only be performed by men, northern Niger.

The festivals can go on for days, the Tinde and Iloughene ceremonies for hours, as can the "Tegbus," a dance generally performed only by men of the blacksmiths clan.

Tuareg men of Teshaq community performing their traditional sword dance.
Timbuktu region, northern Mali.

Tuareg man from Kogo fixing his elaborately wrapped double turban. He is using a water can for his stool and has a mirror to guide himself on his knee. Issaouane/Kogo region, Air Mountains, Niger.

Tuareg men from the mountain oasis of Timia, in full ceremonial regalia, performing the Spear Dance.   Air Mountains, northern Niger.

CHAPTER EIGHT

THE GIFT OF HIS FATHER'S SWORD

It was October, 2000 and I had a full group of Turtle Tours Travelers for the Nomadic Festivals trip to Niger, where we would visit the "Cure Salee" or Salt Cure festivals of the nomadic Tuareg and the Wodaabe tribes.

Our timing was perfect. These annual festivals take place from September through October after the long awaited annual rainy season which usually begins in June and continues through August. The festivals are held in the Azouas region west of Agadez, a sandy Saharan town and the administrative center of the Tuareg North. At this time the land becomes alive with nomads...on the move, at wells, at camps, all in a festive mood. The reason for this is that the earth of the Azouas is very salinated and a heavy monsoon-like rainy season produces an overabundance of luscious super healthy salinated grass for all the animals to eat. At the same time natural ponds form and fill up with richly saturated salinated water.

Wodaabe cattle drinking at a salinated waterhole created by the summer rains.

The urgency to get oneself and one's herds to the Azouas to partake of all this salination is simple. During the nine drought-ridden months preceding the summer rains the nomads' herds of camels, cattle, sheep and goats endure salt deprivation and dehydration, becoming thinner and weaker as the drought continues on, ultimately decimating both pasturage and once-full waterholes. The life-giving capacity of salt is that it traps water in the cells of the body. Imbibing and ingesting the salt restores the health of the animals, hence the name, the "Salt Cure" given to both the event and its concurrent celebrations. This is certainly reason enough to troop your herds into the heart of the region, if keeping them alive is one of your priorities.

   My group and I felt a similar urgency to get there too, although our interest had more to do with anthropology and photography than animal husbandry. We had 12 days on land in which to find and see a festival...or two...maybe even three. Many festivals would be taking place over the two month period as the different lineages and clans of both nomadic groups gathered to put on their own. It's an especially good time for birth celebrations and marriages and both the Wodaabe and Tuareg nomads celebrate in uniquely colorful, traditional ways. Each festival goes on for several days so the chance of learning about one in progress and then driving like bats out of hell to get there before it ended was a good one. It was an issue of being in the right place at the right time.

*Tuareg camels and their calves drinking and bathing in a recently rain-
created water hole, Agadez region, northern Niger.*

   I rendezvoused with my Turtle travelers in Paris and flew south together into Niger along with my French Tour Manager, Christiane Blanc. We flew directly from Paris to Agadez in an abominably uncomfortable charter flight crammed to the gills with French tourists, each also seeking a unique encounter with the Sahara desert. The plane made a quick stop en route at Sabha, a tiny desert airstrip in the heart of the Libyan Sahara to drop off those French passengers who had chosen Libya over Niger as their current Sahara destination.

Tuareg cameleer with his camels loaded with baggage for the 40 day trek to the salt pans of Bilma and Fachi. Sahara desert, northern Niger.

This tiny airport with its mud brick building, plopped down in the middle of glorious pink dunes, was almost mythical and a wonderful presage of vistas awaiting us in the glorious sand dunes to be found in northern Niger's portion of the Sahara.

Drop offs concluded, we continued on to historic Agadez, a small lively town in the Niger Sahara. The color of the surrounding sand, this small town has an appealing market and an unusual mosque dominated by its unique minaret. Agadez and its mosque were founded in the early 15th century by the Tuaregs of the Air Mountains and it quite quickly became the capital of the region. With the development of Islam in the Air it also became a holy city, known especially for its multitude of festivals, primarily religious, of course.

Agadez is also one of the points of departure for the "Azalai." This refers to the Tuareg camel caravans which for centuries have traveled east annually on an 80 day round trip trek across a totally barren, grueling stretch of desert known as the Tenere. Their destination: the salt producing oases of Bilma and Fachi, where the Tuareg trade the various goods they've hauled on their camels, like dried vegetables from their gardens and cloth from the market for the most precious commodity of salt.

Camel caravan en route to northeastern Niger where it will trade local goods for salt.

During the months of November and December it is quite usual for most families to have at least one or two of the menfolk "gone fishin" or in Tuareg terms, "gone Azalai." And let me tell you, this is no "fun weekend away." It gives full meaning to the terms "arduous" and "safety in numbers." There is no "going it alone." Families often join together to make the camel caravan a big one so there are adequate resources. The Tenere is flat as a pancake, with nothing on the horizon for 360 degrees. Nothing, but absolutely nothing, to relieve your eyes. It is just plod, plod, plod, one foot after another for 40 days with an occasional hop up on one of the camels for some relief.

There's even a special camel perfectly designed for the trip...the "utility van" of the camel world. The breed is called Azaragh. These camels come in white with black and brown spots, kind of like a pinto horse. Their special trademark is their very blue eyes. They are mostly deaf and blind, so nothing spooks them. No spitting or biting. They just docilely plod, plod, plod along with the menfolk. It's easy to understand how in its heyday about 700 years ago, one pound of salt was traded for one pound of gold.

Arrival in Agadez by plane used to be an adventure in itself when the airstrip was the same as the one road in and out of town. As we descended we would see the locals still chasing off the tarmac happily grazing donkeys and goats as well as itinerant vehicles. "Customs"

The salt pans of Fachi. The salt is retrieved from the earth through a process of evaporation and then put in molds to solidify. northeastern Sahara, Niger.

itself in the tiny airport was generally perfunctory. We had nothing to declare except the personal ownership of a duffle bag or two. Then we all piled into the Toyota Land Cruisers indicated to drive us to our hotel in town, the Hotel de l'Air, two miles away.

Hotel and dinner arrangements were quickly resolved including baggage distribution and room assignments by Christiane Blanc who always accompanied me as second guide on this trip. Christiane is a Parisian artist who lives full time in her studio in Paris. We first met in 1986 in the Algerian Sahara on my reconnaissance trip for Turtle Tours. She was guiding a tour for a French company. We liked each other immediately. Christiane had studied business management but dropped out quickly to follow her own artistic expression as an "installation" artist. She also has an undying passion for the Sahara.

No matter where she is Christiane always looks and dresses like an artist. She has short closely cropped black hair, and while in the bush on tour usually wears a small turban bound around her head. In Africa she wears long loose African pants she has made in Agadez with big shirts and an ascot always tied around her neck. At the same time she always has her notebook handy to jot down any pertinent information.

Christiane is one of those left brain/right brain people….I mean, one who can be totally creative while still being an excellent manager. Everything about her says " I am an artist but I can run this tour completely so don't worry about a thing." And so people didn't. And neither did I. Christiane was great, super competent and a huge help to me!

The famous Hotel de l'Air where we were spending the night, like all other Agadez buildings, was built of adobe made from the surrounding sand and its "skin color" matched the skin color of every other building in town. It is both fabulously historic and rundown. It was the former palace of the Agadez Sultan but the only thing still palatial about it today are its three-foot thick walls and the cavernous reception room in which breakfast, lunch and coffee are served. To put it precisely, it is shabby, with rickety and noisy old air conditioners, toilets whose seats have long ago cracked or fallen off, showers with trickles of hot and cold water, bathrooms without shower curtains and creaky beds with lumpy pillows and mattresses stuffed with wads of something or other. With only three hotel nights during the entire trip, it really wasn't a big deal. Our goal was to hang out with nomads and you can't do that staying in hotels.

The hotel does have some redeeming features, so let me not pan it completely. It is in the very center of town where there are lots of antiques and souvenir shops. And, the famous Agadez mosque with its unique minaret is right around the corner.

The hotel also has a big terrace on the second floor which has great views of Agadez and is a perfect place for dinner. We eagerly trotted up the thick adobe stairs to the terrace where we gobbled up our dinners of couscous and watermelon. A reasonable red wine provided good solace for the other more faulty conditions. Then it was off to bed, no doubt with our heads full of visions of Sugar Plum Festivals, dancing nomads and prancing camels.

Swords and Turbans:
the two most important elements of
a Tuareg man's costume!

Tuareg man from Kogo in typical festival
dress with traditional sword.

2 Tuareg men from the Air Mountains in
daily garb, also wearing their swords.
Note the difference in turban styles, which
vary from region to region.

Using Agadez as our point of departure, the Nomadic Festivals trip was divided into two sections, with another overnight stay in Agadez in between. The first section including five days among the Wodaabe nomads would take place in the Sahel region of Niger south of Agadez. This is a border of scrubland between the Sahara desert and the more lush, green Savannah. The Sahel, not yet Sahara desert but too arid for most of the farming populations of Niger, provides excellent pasturage for the nomadic cattle-herding Wodaabe. Hopefully we would encounter at least one of their special Gerewol and Worso festivals in honor of the Salt Cure before returning to Agadez for our second hotel overnight.

The second section of the trip was dedicated to our visits among the Tuareg nomads who hosted their own unique celebrations. We would head north and east deeper into the Sahara, traveling up through the Tuareg stronghold of the Air Mountains and touching its borders with the vast Tenere desert. It was five days to be filled with visits to nomadic camps, verdant oases, undulating dunes, rock formations and ancient rock engravings, as well as TurtleWill schools, wells and cooperative projects and, of course, Tuareg Cure Salé festivals, if we could find one.

Christiane had everything well organized for the following morning's departure and the first day out of our overland expedition: 7am wake up call; breakfast at 7:30am of omelets and French bread (a legacy left behind by the French who colonized most of West Africa); and bags and us outside the doors for pick up at 8am! We all assembled in the courtyard and were now ready to hit the road. All we needed were our vehicles and drivers.

We heard the honking of horns outside in the street. We watched with anticipation as the ancient hotel guardian, dressed in an equally ancient faded, pale blue caftan with the ragged cloth of his white turban draped over his shoulders, lifted himself out of his even more ancient chair and shuffled over to open the large double red metal doors of the courtyard. They swung wide with an impressive creak and in drove our four Toyota Land Cruisers.

Our Tuareg drivers jumped out to greet me and Christiane and to be introduced to all the people going with us. They were each shiny clean, all spruced up for the first day of our expedition wearing their traditional black "sarrouel" baggy pants, Tuareg leather sandals on their feet, knee-length tunics in varying shades of blue, and black or white turbans carefully wrapped around their heads. None of them felt the need to veil their faces in the traditional Tuareg way because they knew that we would be journeying together and living side-by-side over the next two weeks and such formality was not necessary.

The only elements missing from their garb were their Tuareg swords or "tacoubas." Every Tuareg, as part of his full traditional dress code, carries a long traditional Tuareg sword. They are fully encased in embossed leather with a strap to hang over the shoulder. The sword is as common to every Tuareg male as is his fifteen feet of turban. A Tuareg and his sword are like a boy and his dog. They are rarely parted. Except, of course, when you're driving an expedition vehicle with a group of tourists. Then you keep it hidden in the trunk.

At first glance everything seemed the same as usual. We had four vehicles, Christiane as second guide, 13 Turtle Tourist travelers, Hima my Tuareg cook of many, many years and the usual four Tuareg drivers. On second glance, however, I realized that there were only three of the usual drivers. There was my lead driver, Bamba, but there was a new Tuareg driver, Ibrahim, whom I had never met before. The four drivers gathered up everyone's baggage, my travelers took their places in the vehicles and we headed out for our first big adventure in search of the Wodaabe Festivals. I always rode in the first vehicle with the lead driver, Christiane followed in the second vehicle, and vehicles three and four followed behind.

The new Tuareg driver Ibrahim was apparently the designated second vehicle driver and so Christiane took her place in the front seat beside him. I couldn't help but notice rather early on that he was truly an anomaly and unlike any other Tuareg I had seen before. He was quite tall and plump, lacking the normal elegance of the sinewy, lean and graceful Tuareg body. What's more, he paid little attention to his appearance, his clothing seemed to hang askew, he always looked completely disheveled and his white turban was most often wrapped haphazardly as if he'd just come out of battle with a head injury and was searching for the first Red Cross unit he could find.

What's worse, he made lots of noise. Each afternoon on arrival at camp he would climb up on the top of his truck to unload the baggage, and heave the mattresses down onto the ground with grunts and shouts. Heave, grunt, shout. Heave, grunt, shout. To top it off, as he bent down to pick up each bag to heave, grunt, and shout it down onto the ground he would bend over a bit too far so that his blue tunic shirt would lift up behind and his baggy sarrouel pants fell down enough to reveal that intimate backside crease that the plumbing profession in America is famous for, but that absolutely no other self-respecting Tuareg, noble or not, would permit to happen. He certainly didn't have the reserve and propriety common to the Tuareg culture.

Ibrahim in Kogo with his son
northern sahara, Niger.

92

Bamba, a Tuareg from Agadez and my lead driver for many years, Agadez, northern Niger.

I should mention here that upon introduction to the Tuareg of Niger, first through Mano Dayak of Temet Voyages and now through Barney of Dunes Voyages, I couldn't help but fall in love with them. They were so open, friendly, hard working, quick to laugh and fun to be with. They had the laughter of West Africa in their hearts. They would always go the extra mile for you, carry the bags for someone who needed help, and just generally were totally willing to assist. Whether they were of noble origin or not was irrelevant. They were there to help. But they still maintained their own personal decorum and "heave, grunt, shout" was not included in that. Oddly enough though, none of the other Tuareg seemed to mind Ibrahim's cultural aberrations. In fact they seemed quite devoted to him.

To make matters worse, he drove Christiane crazy. The four vehicles were supposed to travel in a single file so that each driver could keep track of the car behind in case it should run into trouble, like a flat tire. But Ibrahim truly had a will of his own. He would pull out of his second place in line to race ahead in tandem with my car, egging my driver on for a race. This was really too much for Christiane who always liked things very orderly, which made her occasionally tough on the staff but a great Tour Manager. Ibrahim's one saving grace was that he sang beautifully and if we chanced to hear him sing Tuareg melodies at night around the campfire we were truly lucky. Whenever we asked him to sing for us he would completely clam up.

By day four Christiane was completely fed up with squabbling with Ibrahim to get him to stay in line and, just basically, do whatever she said. He didn't like her anymore than she liked him. He found her bossy. She found him a pain in the butt. As we were returning to Agadez the following morning for visits in town and our second hotel overnight before starting our next five days among the Tuareg she now asked me to talk to Barney about replacing Ibrahim with another driver. Barney is French and had been Mano Dayak's partner at Temet voyages. After Mano's death in the plane accident Barney opened his own agency called Dunes Voyages.

Once back in Agadez I went to see Barney. First on the agenda was to give him a report of our past week in the bush. The time among the Wodaabe was a big hit and all that we had hoped for. Our second day out we came across a festival in full swing. This was a traditional "Gerewol" festival in which two lineages came together to visit, share news and above all to compete in the male beauty contest, known as the "Gerewol." The two lineages were the Bii Nga'en and the Gojanko'en, among whom I had many friends.

A large flat area in the bush had been designated so that many families from each lineage could set up temporary households together with their herds. Our days were filled with visits among the various families, admiring the "sagas" which are the traditional displays of each Wodaabe woman's personal wealth including all her personally and ornately decorated calabashes, tin plates and charmingly colorful bedsteads. Each woman is very proud of her possessions and her ability to make a grand and artistic display. During the course of the year preceding the festivals the Wodaabe are on the move constantly so the women keep the contents of their sagas carefully wrapped up to prevent any breakage. It is only at festival time that all her treasures are unwrapped and shared for viewing in such a mass way. The air is literally palpable with the shared joy, pride and admiration among all the women.

Traditional Wodaabe woman's display of her best and most precious possessions...akin to western usage of a china cabinet. Displays like this are only set out when the women are at big festivals and gatherings such as the "Worso" which is the traditional annual reunion of a sub-lineage.
Lineages are similar to clans, all members being descendants of one ancestor.

In the early afternoon the young men start preparing their astounding yellow, black and white facial makeup and matching traditional costumes of ornately embroidered tunics, In the early afternoon the young men start preparing their astounding yellow, black and white facial makeup and matching traditional costumes of ornately embroidered tunics, leather bottom wrappers and strands of white beads criss-crossing their chests. All this is topped by their completely made up faces and white turbans, graced with ostrich plumes and long dangling brass covered earrings. We wandered from shady spot to shady spot where we could watch them getting ready under the shelter of trees.

The Yaake competition itself starts around 4 PM. The men all line up shoulder to shoulder holding each other's hands, swaying and stepping back and forth to the hypnotic rhythm of a repetitive four-syllable chant "ah um ah la, ah um ah la, ah um ah la, ah um ah la." In the meanwhile they roll their eyes and wiggle their lips, just exactly like you see on all the National Geographic documentaries. This was the real thing and we were all in National Geographic heaven. The contest goes on for hours while all the available young women, dressed in their finest, watch in their own line from a distance. Eventually the winners are picked by the three young women deemed the most beautiful.

Wodaabe men in full traditional Yaake costume for the Beauty Competition
Azouas region, northern Niger.
For more about the Wodaabe, see page 11 and chapters 10-12.

Next on my agenda in Agadez to discuss with Barney were the details for our second week in the bush with the Tuareg, and now also about Ibrahim. "Barney," I said. "I've got a problem. This new driver you put on the trip acts and looks less like any Tuareg I've ever met before. He's noisy, headstrong, and looks like he just escaped from a hospital ward. He is creating a real problem with Christiane and she doesn't want him as her driver anymore. Can you find me another driver?"

Barney was totally dismayed. He said, "I'm really sorry to hear you say that because I put him on the trip specifically for reasons of security. He was the leader of the rebel army. There's a lot of banditry going on in the bush where you're going and Ibrahim is very well known by all the Tuareg. He's loved and respected by all, including bandits, and I suggest that you keep him. He'll keep you safe."

"Ooops," I thought. It took me less than a nano-second to respond. "Oh, right, Barney! Sure thing, No problem. Absolutely 100% A-OK. Ibrahim stays on the trip. Christiane will just have to make do. Or, she can ride with another driver."

Christiane's nano-second matched mine. She quickly acquiesced. She and Ibrahim made a silent and peaceful pact to work together. It was an easy week in the bush without any problems. We drove through the fascinatingly rugged and rocky scenery of the Air Mountains visiting Tuareg communities where we were funding schools, cooperatives and wells. Every day the locals put on festivals for us. We were treated like royalty for all the humanitarian aid Turtle Tours and TurtleWill had been giving. (For photos of Tuareg Festivals see pages 74-83.)

For our last night camping out in the desert in a beautiful spot of dunes Ibrahim had promised to sing for us. I figured he'd spend 20 minutes or so singing lots of different Tuareg melodies but, no, he sang only one and that was it. Up he clammed once again. The party was over.

The next day was our last day in the bush and after our picnic lunch we held our usual special ceremony of thanks for all the staff. We gave them their tips and made funny little jokes and everybody shook hands and hugged their favorite drivers and said what a great trip they had had. The expedition leader Bamba made a little speech about what good travelers everyone was and how easy they had all been to work with and then he announced that another one of the staff wanted to say something special on his own.

Ibrahim stepped forward and said that he was deeply touched by the generosity, the kindness and the caring for his people that he witnessed and that he had never before seen white people act like that. Normally white people just traveled through, took their pictures and left. But we actually stuck around to see what was needed to help and then to implement. He thanked us all on behalf of the Tuareg.

That evening I went over to my truck to get something out of the front seat. Ibrahim's vehicle was parked to the right of mine and he came over to get something out of his front seat so we were positioned side-by-side. I reached over, touched his arm and said "Ibrahim,

Ibrahim Bareghi ready for a festival.

Photos of Ibrahim by Carol Carpenter

In Memoriam
Ibrahim died in his natal desert of Kogo in 2011

thank you so much for your words today. They meant so much to me." He turned to me and he said, "I know I was kind of difficult at the beginning of the trip and that you asked Barney to replace me. I'm sorry for any trouble I might've caused, especially to Christiane."

Then, he reached inside his truck and he drew out a long "Tacouba," the traditional Tuareg sword in its original leather casing with shoulder strap. He showed me the sword and shyly said to me, "this was my father's sword and I want you to have it." Then he got kind of stumbley and embarrassed and said "Now I'm giving it to you so it is yours. If you don't want to keep it you can give it away, but now it's yours." Then he drew it out of the case to show me how sharp it was and how to handle it with care so I wouldn't hurt myself. I was honored and touched beyond words. It is still the most precious gift I have ever received from anyone.

That night at dinner at the local restaurant back in Agadez I told everyone the story of who he was, why he was on the trip and that he had given me his father's sword. One of the ladies on the tour said she had seen him get up early in the morning, and climb the dune we were camped next to, wearing the sword. She said he stayed up there for quite a while by himself seated on top of the dune and holding the sword in his lap. My intuition tells me that he was communing with his deceased father explaining to him how and why he was passing the sword onto me.

Ibrahim is a noble Tuareg from Kogo Issaouane, one of the farthest out Tuareg communities of nomads in Niger. His lineage and family have lived there for centuries in a region of spectacular dunes, some of which are dotted with huge pieces of blue marble. There is no water. The nearest well is 25 kilometers away. Many people including Mano Dayak have tried to dig wells for the nomads of Kogo but all the wells have failed. In 2012 TurtleWill succeeded in digging Issaouane a well. Water was reached at 100 feet. Of the 53 wells dug by TurtleWill this was for me the most important, dug in honor of Ibrahim's father-in-law, Ebeghar Ewindighi, a very highly respected patriarch of his tribe and lineage, and for Ibrahim Bareghi, a champion of his people.

IN MEMORIAM
1995
Mano Dayak: Leader of the Tuareg Rebellion in Niger

Mano Dayak, an old friend who first ran our Sahara Desert Tours in Niger, and then took over the leadership of the Tuareg Rebellion in Niger in 1993, died in an airplane explosion in November, 1995 on his way to a meeting with the Prime Minister for final negotiations of the peace settlement. Mano was a true hero to his people, an international spokesman for their cause, and a very special human being.

Here I am in 1988 on my first trip with Temet Voyages, owned by Mano Dayak and "Barney" Bernard Raymond. After Mano's death Barney created a new agency called Dunes Voyages with which I have continued to work since then.

The man in the center is "Hima," my cook of many, many years. Hima could make the most wondrous meals out of sand and camel butter!

My first trip to the Niger Sahara in 1988.

CHAPTER NINE

THE STORY OF FATI GAMBO

It was March, 2002. Fati Gambo had been waiting at the Tuareg village of Tamazalak, in the Air Mountains, northern Niger, for two days to meet me. She had a baby at her breast and another three-year-old running in circles around her feet. She was dressed like all the other Tuareg ladies, in the traditional loose white blouse with black starbursts of embroidery, and a black wrapper skirt. I knew she wasn't Tuareg, though, because her facial and body features were soft and round, and not angular and sinewy, which is the Tuareg norm. She was Haussa, a member of the dominant Black African group in Niger. She was at that point recently divorced from a Tuareg from Tamazalak.

Fati had completed her training in computer skills and had heard that I might be opening an office in the town of Agadez for TurtleWill. She wanted desperately to work for me. She had just traveled three days on a donkey with her children to Tamazalak to wait for my arrival. I explained that I wouldn't be opening an office in Agadez because TurtleWill projects all took place in the bush, like the women's basketry cooperative at Tamazalak that we were there to visit. Fati promptly announced that she had other skills as well. She could teach the women how to use a sewing machine, how to knit, even how to read and write! Alhousseini Biki, the Tuareg educator who runs all TurtleWill projects in Niger, confirmed that these seemed like great opportunities. The women could make clothes for themselves as well as sell them to others. The knitting would be also really useful. A cold spell that winter had given all the children respiratory infections because they had nothing warm to wear. As for reading and writing classes, we should ask the women.

At our campsite in a nearby dry river bed that night we all agreed that Fati had excellent ideas. The ultimate decisions would be up to the Tamazalak women whom we would see the next day.

The next morning we stopped first at the new local dispensary which the government had just built for Tamazalak. This was actually a tiny two room cement block building. The first room was the "reception" sporting a large metal cabinet with the most minimal selection of medicines, mostly a few jars of mebendazole for deworming, some bottles of alcohol and less than 10 boxes of cotrimoxazole, otherwise known as bactrim and one of the drugs of choice in West Africa. There was also a wooden desk with a large notebook sitting on top, hungrily waiting for patients to be formally inscribed inside, and two chairs. The second room was the examining room and contained a large and harsh metal examination table and a peculiar baby's scale which looked more suited to a green grocer's produce than a medical clinic. The nurse in charge told me that they needed a midwife to help them with their female patients. Perhaps we could find one in the community?

From here we went on to the schoolhouse. Waiting for us were the chief of the village and a few other important male members of the community. Fati Gambo and Ghaisha Abardak, the president of the Tamazalak Basketry Cooperative TurtleWill had recently funded soon arrived with several other women. I proposed Fati's Sewing and Knitting workshop and they all loved it. I explained that TurtleWill would fund the machines and the first round of materials, but after that they would have to purchase all materials themselves. They agreed. Next we discussed Fati's proposal to teach them to read and write. There was a hearty response including requests to bring their children to class who weren't doing so well in school. Kaywela Amoumoune announced that she should teach the reading and writing class because she had previously done this at Tamazalak. Everyone confirmed. They also readily agreed to instruction on family and household hygiene, another one of Fati's offerings. Such wise women.

The last question was if there were anyone at Tamazalak to do the midwife training program at the hospital in Agadez. Fatima Abardak was immediately chosen.

As a final comment, I told them that I wanted them all to take a good look at Fati Gambo, because it was due to her courage and absolute insistence upon seeing me that all these projects were happening. Fati had come looking for a job for herself and had ended up benefiting a host of people. My point was not just that they should thank her, but that they should learn from her example, that any one of them could accomplish what she had in mind, just like Fati Gambo. Ghaisha responded saying that they had already gained a new sense of self and security thanks to the basketry cooperative and the money they were each able to make. With that they all stood up and prepared to walk out.

"Do you see that!" Alhousseini exclaimed. "According to our tradition, if a woman is seated among men, she is never allowed to stand up to leave if the men are still seated. She must wait, even all afternoon if necessary and even if the children are starving at home, until the men stand up and thus give her permission to leave. And now, right here, all our women have just stood up on their own without our permission and are leaving!"

There was a mixture of both amusement and admiration as he said this. None of the other men seemed to take offense. Clearly the Tamazalak women had reached a new level of self-empowerment.

Fati Gambo concluded by saying that she had come all that way desperately looking for a job for herself and now she was going to be helping a lot of other women. This meant so much to her, she didn't care if she didn't get paid at all.

The Sewing and Knitting workshop was launched with 35 women enrolled in the three-month program. Fatima Abardark was promptly enrolled in the Midwife training program in Agadez and Kaywela Moumoumoune's three month Adult Education classes started up immediately, all funded by TurtleWill!

TurtleWill's Cooperatives programs in Niger, which grew so rapidly because of Fati Gambo, included 106 micro-credit food co-ops, sewing and handicrafts co-ops, plus adult literacy programs. They have empowered over 6,000 women. It's an amazing legacy. We are all so grateful to Fati Gambo and the stunning example that she set!

Ghaissa Abardek, president of the Tamazalak Basketry Co-op and I in 2002
Tamazalak community, Air Mountains, northern Niger.

Tagaza Sewing Cooperative, northern Niger.

Women's Handicrafts Cooperative, Asharane community. The women work with goat skins primarily and make these beautiful cushions, purses and other leather goods. Goundam region, northern Mali.

First encounters with the local women, 1988

Tenilet Food Cooperative, Tamazalak region, Air Mountains, northern Niger.

Kaywela Amoumoune (on the left) teaching adult literacy. Tamazalak, Air Mountains,Niger.

CHAPTER TEN

LEARNING THE WODAABE WAY

Gundi Bazay is a chief of the Bii Nga'en lineage of Wodaabe nomads of the Republic of Niger. Most people know of the Wodaabe as the tribe whose men paint their faces for those bizarre male beauty contests, the "Yaake," in which they roll their eyes, wiggle their lips and flash their teeth. This is a competition to choose the most beautiful male, as judged by the most beautiful young women. This was how I first met Chief Gundi in 1989. I was in northern Niger in the InGall region with a group of Turtle Travelers, precisely to see these festivals.

Gundi, however, was not painted, so it was not his rolling eyes that got me. He just looked fantastic, dressed in full chief regalia, from head to toe in black, a la Tuareg. In this part of the world, which is the Sahel region bordering on the edges of the Sahara desert, all the men tend to adopt the dress of the Tuareg. It's the most suited for the climate, what with its loose flowing robes, and it sure looks great at a party.

Gundi and I took a liking to each other immediately, but much to my disappointment, he had to rush back into the bush to his family after the celebrations. As a chief, he was not there to participate but to oversee his troops and their festivities. He invited me to come back to see him, at another time, when I could spend a few days with him and his family in the bush, and he would teach me all about "the Wodaabe Way." An invitation I could hardly pass up, but when to do it was another question. So we parted, he to return to his family, and I to lead my group onto yet another group of Wodaabe at their festivals in InGall.

The Wodaabe, ancient nomadic cattle herders of the Sahel, live and roam primarily in Niger and the northern part of Nigeria. Their goal in life is nothing more than to walk in front of their herds. As nomads, they live isolated in the bush in tiny units of one or two families for the nine dry months of the year, moving every two or three days in search of water and pasturage. Following their own centuries old ancestral migration routes which usually guarantees a working well every now and then, they criss-cross occasionally with other families. Even their herds, composed of Bororoji long-horned cattle of Asian origin, are unique. If you think Texan long-horn cattle have big horns, you should see the heads of horns on these Wodaabe cattle.

The Wodaabe are a subgroup of the much bigger group of West African herders, the Fulani or Peul, and speak the same language of Fulfulde. As a tightly knit subgroup, the Wodaabe have almost never married outside their own lineage and so have maintained a very pure body type and facial structure. They consider themselves very handsome. They're right. The Wodaabe, being neither Caucasian nor Negroid but a race apart, really do stand out from the rest of the indigenous populations of Black Africa. Both men and women have facial tattoos, indicating their lineage. They are often thought to be of ancient Ethiopian origin or one of the lost tribes of Israel.

Wodaabe chief Gundi Bazay, one of the chiefs of the Bii Nga'en lineage.
Agadez region, northern Niger.

The women can be exceedingly beautiful with their coppery brown skin and very fine chiseled features. As for the men, their faces are handsome and more rugged than the more even-featured Tuareg. You can differentiate at once between Wodaabe and Tuareg men if a Wodaabe man is turbanless. This often happens, since for him the turban is a convenience and not the cultural regulation that it is for the Tuareg. Once a Tuareg male reaches puberty he dons the turban and it will never come off in public. Wodaabe men are much more cavalier about their turbans, so you often see them bare-headed and their hair done up in traditional Wodaabe braids. Just like their women, they all wear their hair in exactly the same style.

Wodaabe woman with traditional hairstyle, earrings and amulets.
Azouas region, northern Niger.

Arriving in InGall, in the northern part of Niger on the edge of the Sahara, we headed off immediately in search of the action. This was how I met Moneidji Gorsay, a chief of the Yamankoe'en lineage. Moneidji immediately invited us to attend his Yaake. Traditionally two lineages compete with each other in these competitions which go on for several days. We joined Moneidji and his group in a grove of trees, where all the young men, "sukaabe," who dared to compete were getting into their costumes and make-up for the Yaake dance.

Wodaabe man putting on his Yaake make up for the Beauty Competition. He is already wearing his special embroidered tunic and his leather "skirt"

Wodaabe make-up is something else. Elizabeth Arden really wouldn't know what to say. Certainly the objective is the same, but the applications are worlds apart.

Wodaabe make-up is designed to enhance what Wodaabe men feel are the most significant aspects of traditional Wodaabe beauty, all of which set them distinctly apart from the surrounding negroid populations.

A yellow-brown tint is spread evenly over the front oval of the face, emphasizing the thin angularity of Wodaabe features and their high foreheads. A lighter decorative stripe is then drawn right down the center of the face from the top of the forehead to the tip of nose, thereby emphasizing their long thin noses. Lips are carefully outlined in black, emphasizing their thin lips and the whiteness of their teeth. Wodaabe really do have very beautiful, very white teeth. Who wouldn't if their diet consisted of milk and millet, Chinese green tea with fluoride and no candy stands and junk food on every corner? Eyes are also outlined in black to make them look whiter when they are rolling them around. The finishing touches to this unique look are colorful stars, circles and lines on the cheek bones and corners of the eyes.

Next comes the costume. The comfortable daily flowing robes of the Tuareg are shed and out comes a finery you would never expect, starting with turbans from which hang long leather earrings bound in brass strips and decorated with cowrie shells. Add to this silver amulets tied on at the forehead and ostrich plumes poking out at the top. Or perhaps the contestant will wear the more typical Fulani cone-shaped hat of leather, to which he may add a decoration or two, such as more ostrich plumes.

Then comes a sleeveless, open-sided, long, narrow, blue tunic, elegantly embroidered in the Wodaabe way with colorful geometric designs and patterns, highlighting muscular arms and sinewy bodies. For pants he wears the traditional Wodaabe leather wrapper, which wraps tightly around his very narrow hips and buttocks (the envy of any woman), and has a long tail in the back that is pulled forward between the legs, hiked up through the waistband and then hangs down decoratively in the front and is embellished with brass and beads. Over all this he wears whatever jewelry he can find, including a variety of gaudy stuff from the local markets as well as the traditional Wodaabe necklaces of brass, leather, cowries and beads, and chokers of tiny leather talismans. On his feet are usually elegant Tuareg handmade thong-style sandals of red and green decorated leather. The finale is the graceful Tuareg sword or "tacouba," which swings elegantly at his side.

Wodaabe Yaake beauty competition in full swing.

All in all, these guys look great, even though at first glance to the average outsider they may look a tad "over the top." The overall objective, immediate and otherwise, is to charm as much of their female population as they can.

"Caye'en," young men of competition age, performing the Yaake dance, each with his own style of decoration, enhancing his own beauty as he sees it!

When each "Cayedjo" (single of Caye 'en) man is ready, he joins the circle of dancers. Men stand tightly side by side, arms from the shoulder to the elbow touching, hands clasped. The group chants, led by one person and punctuated with syncopated clapping. The song, composed of a few monosyllabic phrases, is repetitive, mesmerizing, hypnotic. The sound is deep and primordial, like a call to the wild. This is alpha state trance-like music, typical of many primitive societies. The dancers sway gently and the circle gradually turns. The motion is slow, an elegant up and down on the toes, a swinging forward of the arms, a step or two forward and backward, a step to the side. It continues, same tonalities, same punctuation, same motion, without stopping for a long time.

Moneidji invited us to join the circle and we were immediately embraced tightly into the group of male dancers. I was quickly caught up in the trance. Being inside the circle next to the men was almost hallucinogenic as the sound of their deep chant-like song enveloped me from three sides. My movements were now their movements and I turned with them in the circle. Every now and then two or three dancers would take short rapid hops into the center of the circle and do a special dancing, clapping movement, then retreat back into the governing circle. We did this also. We felt honored at being part of this ancient ritual. It was more than thrilling. It was like being in a time warp. It was surreal.

The young "Surbaabe" Wodaabe women of the competing lineage who had come to InGall for the festivals stood off to the side in a tight line, carefully watching the dancers without letting their interest show. Women are not supposed to look at what they like. They also had on all their finery including their best embroidered tunics and skirts and all the brass, leather and beaded jewelry they owned. On top of their heads they carried another folded piece of traditional Wodaabe cloth, made of woven strips of heavy blue material. This was not only their sun protection. This served also as the mat they use for sitting or lying on the ground.

The "Gerewol" term refers to both the overall festival and a specific form of dance. This dance we had been invited to join is the "Ruume," done shoulder to shoulder in a tight circle. Each man can make up and costume himself as he chooses. The "Yaake" dance is always done in a long line so observers can watch and judge. This is the one that makes all the Off-Broadway headlines and National Geographic documentaries, where the men wear yellow and black face paint, do indeed wiggle their lips, click their tongues, make kissing sounds, flash their teeth and roll their eyes. This is the Charm contest and it is judged by the women of the competing lineage. To the Wodaabe women this is charm at its zenith.

The "Gerewol" competition is quite different. The men are judged on beauty alone, so all their make-up and costumes are "regulation," the same red face paint, white beads, white costumes. No personal creativity is allowed. The Gerewol is also done in a line and judged by the most beautiful young women of the day. I find it more elegant and haunting than the Yaake.

As all the young girls who have come to see the performance stand apart in their own lines at a distance from the men, the three most beautiful girls are selected by the elders in charge of these rituals to be the judges of the competition. These young women must do a ritual dance of their own which leads them towards the male dancers in a shuffling single file, eyes averted, one arm held gracefully up in the air while the other hand is held against the cheek. At the indicated moment, each one walks slowly toward her choice and almost touches him, but not quite. (see page 13) The three male winners are then pulled out of the line and they are paraded around in a similar winning shuffle. Congratulations are the same the world over.

Soon enough it was time for me and my group to head back to camp. As we were getting ready to go Moneidji extended to me that very same invitation, word for word, that Gundi had…to come back for a few days and stay with him and his family in the bush, and he would teach me the Wodaabe Way. Was this the Wodaabe line, or what?

Surbaabe, young women of marriageable age.

Now that I had two invitations from chiefs to return to the bush and Learn the Wodaabe Way, I decided I'd better get going on this important and tantalizing opportunity!!!

Young Surbaabe Gerewol watchers.

My curiosity had gotten the best of me and I was one step ahead, having already picked up some pointers on what exactly is the Wodaabe Way.

For one thing, it is that the women do the choosing. Wodaabe men can have up to four wives, but if you ask them how they got them, you will usually discover that it was the women who chose them. The first marriage or "koobgal" is an arranged one, set up by parents at a very early age, but for the rest, "teegal" or love marriages, you are on your own. A Wodaabe woman is free to choose whomever she wants, and free to leave whenever she wants as well. The one drawback is that she must leave all her children behind except those who are under seven years old. Her ex-husband will claim them when they reach seven. These festivals are thus the source of new marriages, alliances and dalliances, because a woman who is no longer happy with her present spouse can choose to leave him if she finds a better option, or just have a short-lived fling. No reprobation or shame is attached.

Note that these "love" marriages are often formed initially and rapidly on the basis of little more than a shared eye contact or fleeting glance. Other than at festival time, the Wodaabe live out in the bush, under very harsh dry season conditions, isolated from one another for 9-10 months of the year. So, this societal flexibility strikes me as a very simple and realistic solution, should a husband's attentions switch too greatly from one wife to another, or the chemistry that initially brought them together wears off a bit too soon. Women have options.

The Wodaabe Way is complicated to say the least, and includes a host of governing taboos, which explains why the Wodaabe call themselves, "People of the Taboo." Taboos, like ritual decoration, fall into the category of insidiously clever psychological manipulation that works well towards keeping a group together. The fear of breaking taboos, due to the resulting mishaps and woes that will befall the individual and the group to which he or she belongs, is so strong that they are rarely defied and the group stays together. Among the Wodaabe, taboos are primal. They govern the way men and women relate to each other and their children, how and when they talk to each other, how the herds are cared for, the days of the month and the weeks they can migrate, how the animals are tied up at night. Engaged children are not allowed to look at each other, married couples cannot hold hands in public, mothers cannot touch their babies at all during the first week of their birth, parents cannot participate in naming ceremonies, and more. Pretty much the gamut of Wodaabe life is reinforced with taboos. Maybe this, combined with their unique customs, dress and nomadic habits, is why and how the Wodaabe remain the Wodaabe.

Despite what appears to be an impossible list of taboos governing behavior between men and women once they are engaged or married, the Wodaabe really do have a great time together. Being with them at a Gerewol festival reminded me of watching puppy dogs at play. Men and women sit around talking together in groups, and every fellow at one point or another seemed to have his head in some lady's lap, getting his hair rebraided for the dances. This is the antithesis of most African societies as I know them, where men sit in one group and women sit in another, with communication kept to a minimum. Not so the Wodaabe. Festival time is the time they wait for all year, and you can bet they enjoy it to the hilt. Bravo, Wodaabe.

Young "Surbaajo" girl (pl: Surbaabe).

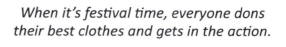

When it's festival time, everyone dons their best clothes and gets in the action.

117

*Gerewol
Competitors.*

Gerewol Competitor's last minute check!

Gerewol Beauty Competition.

Surbaajo girl enjoying the day.

CHAPTER ELEVEN

IN SEARCH OF GUNDI

I returned to Niger the following summer of 1990, this time with just two other people, Ann and Marta, both of whom had been on so many previous trips with me that we had our traveling styles down pat. This was not going to be any official Turtle Tour with set itinerary. We would just head out into the bush to see what we could find. I, of course, knew exactly what I had in mind to find, and Marta and Ann were willing accomplices. We were off, in search of Gundi. We were accepting his offer. We wanted to visit him and his family, live in the bush and learn more about the Wodaabe Way.

Gundi Bazay, a chief of the Bii Nga'en lineage of the Wodaabe tribe, northern Niger.

I had been corresponding with Gundi during the previous year, his letters to me written by his literate friend, the tailor. The letters were simple, mostly with news of his herds and his family. So, I knew more or less where to find Gundi and he knew more or less that I was coming. Biano, one of my favorite Tuareg drivers, and Hima, my cook, met us at the Niamey airport and we left immediately. The grand search for Gundi had now officially begun.

800 kilometers of smooth, asphalted highway due north and then with a sudden abrupt left turn we barreled directly into the bush, leaving behind what remained of civilization... or was it sanity...to now follow what remained of the old road to InGall. Gundi and his Bii Nga'en Wodaabe would be somewhere out there. We bumped along over indescribable turf for the first two days, stopping at every Wodaabe camp we could find, asking for the whereabouts of one chief Gundi. The first groups didn't know Gundi, but at least could tell us that the Bii Nga'en were way, way further north. Ancient annual ancestral migration routes are always maintained, so at any given time of the year a family can be located within a radius or 10-50 miles.

By the morning of the third day, we were getting a bit weary of this bumping, stopping, asking; bumping, stopping, asking. Added to this was a fair amount of digging because the rainy season had left the dirt tracks we were following nearly impassable and we often found ourselves mired in mud. Biano and Hima responded with the patience of saints as they dug us out time after time.

Biano by now felt it was his personal obligation to get me to Gundi. Biano was a big-bellied wise old sage of a Tuareg, about 60 plus years old, with almost no hair under his turban and missing a similar amount of teeth. But Biano certainly knew what he was doing because who should we literally run into later that very afternoon but Gundi's younger brother, Kabo, who had been off at a Gerewol in the neighboring bush with some friends. They had traveled there by camel and were now returning to the home camp. Kabo was incredulous at finding me. So were we! Had it been five minutes earlier or later our paths would never have crossed! Kabo leapt off his camel, quickly tossed the reins to one of his friends and jumped into our truck to lead us "direct" to Gundi. But this was just another example of the "Wodaabe Way." "Direct to Gundi" in Wodaabe talk meant many, many more kilometers and several hours more of this inexorable driving and bumping. At least the "asking" was over.

Hallelujah. At 8PM we were told to stop and make camp at the edge of what, in the thick darkness, looked like impenetrable bush. Hima made dinner, we put up our tents, and Kabo left us to find Gundi, who was camped, as they say in Wodaabe, "right over there." Midnight. Finally voices and footsteps. Gundi and Kabo had arrived. Yes, he really was right over there with his family and herds. About 10 kilometers away, as the crow walks, and that is just what Gundi and his brother had done, albeit quickly. By now I was the only one up to greet them, along with a million stars.

The next morning after everyone had awakened, Marta and Ann met Gundi. Truly an impressive chief, they agreed. We agreed also that we would join his family out on their Wodaabe manoeuvres, so Kabo went ahead to tell them where to meet us for that evening's camp. We headed out by car, and Gundi's family continued on by foot from the campsite where they were the night before. With them went all their herd of cattle, donkeys, sheep and goats. All their goods were loaded on to the donkeys and pack oxen. Some of the women rode donkeys, but most simply walked alongside.

We arrived first at the designated site, which was further along the edge of that huge grassy pastureland that had looked like impenetrable bushy terrain in the darkness the night before. Wow! It looked like every nomad and his cousin, including Wodaabe and Tuareg, were camped out there because it was just after the rains, and the grass was about as rich and lush as it could be. Because we had the vehicle we couldn't risk driving in to join them, as we would, with total certainty, get stuck in the mud. We had already dug ourselves out of many 2-foot holes often enough on this journey, and none of us were in the mood to do it again. Not that we three ladies had been allowed to pitch in, but it did take a lot of fortitude to watch. We camped instead on the hard rocky ground bordering the pastureland.

We set up our camp and eventually Gundi's family arrived. The family consisted of several women, many children and a smattering of men, as each man, according to the Wodaabe way, can have up to four wives for himself. The herds had been taken into the pastureland so their camp was quickly unloaded from their donkeys. Camp consisted of several beds, and that was it.

Wodaabe wives Matka and Nyali of Chief Tambari Girka of the Behame'en lineage, with children and donkeys.

Rhodo, first wife of Chief Moneidji Gorsay, with an Elletel that she is finishing for me!

   The Wodaabe don't sleep in tents or shelters and wonder why others do. Each Wodaabe "homestead" consists of two "platforms," one of which is more bed-like and made out of large bed-length wooden spools across which several slats or sticks are placed. Reed mats are placed on top of this and presto, you have your bed, your home, your kingdom. Easy to set up, dismantle and pack up.

Wodaabe can be on the go within the hour, and as nomads, they usually are, every other day or so. They would not dream of disrespecting the pre-determined days which are favorable for travel and those which are taboo.

Each married Wodaabe woman has two of these structures, one she uses for sleeping purposes and one she uses to display her traditional "saga," or trousseau. This consists primarily of her "calabashes" or gourds, each personally and ornately decorated by herself with Wodaabe designs; colorfully decorated aluminum plateware she has purchased in the market, often with a portrait of the president of the country on them; and her reed mats for sleeping. This is how she measures her wealth. A Wodaabe man measures his in cattle, but he will never tell you how many he has. Out of pure superstition, he will tell you he's not sure.

Saga with two Elletels but no Kakols. Note that most items are still in their travel packaging so we can't tell what other treasures are contained here. Only those needed for daily use are visible as the photo was not taken at festival time.

In addition, each Wodaabe woman's saga contains at least one "Elletel," and a larger size "Kakol." These are very important, odd, phallic-looking objects, which identify the household as a Wodaabe home. They remind me of Jewish Mazuzahs which identify a Jewish home. They are covered with string and the silver foil retrieved from the inside of powdered milk boxes, and have who knows what stuffed inside, probably grasses and rags. Anything else the family owns, which is usually nothing more than a few wooden bowls and garments, are stored also on the second bed.

Very beautiful saga with several Kakols.

During the "Worso" celebrations, which are the huge annual family reunions of a sublineage, the men get to show off their herds and the women get to show off their own wealth, as in their sagas. Each woman polishes and repairs all her calabashes and puts them out on exhibit, along with her Elletels and Kakols, as part of a group display. Imagine a long line of 30-40 Wodaabe beds, each one resplendent with these objects. The ultimate Wodaabe Tupperware party. All the women come to admire and judge and the winners are celebrated in song.

So there we were, with our combined camp stretching out at a great distance, as the beds were lined up one after the other, and not in a circle as one might have imagined. No need apparently to circle the wagons. The first beds all belonged to Gundi's immediate family

including wives and mother, in some kind of pecking order. Way, way out at the end and with a certain distance from the others, was a solitary pair of beds. These belonged to Gundi's sister-in-law who preferred her privacy.

When a man has several wives, the question of where he spends each night is handled democratically, on a fair and square rotation basis. The Wodaabe are Muslim, which only permits four wives, but for the Wodaabe, it's different. If another woman wants to join the team, why not? "Where there is couscous for one, there is couscous for ten."

Unlike the Tuareg who always sleep in tents, occasionally in the rainy season some Wodaabe will build a tent-like structure out of mats on top of the bed, but most often the Wodaabe

Pirogi Daneri, a Behame'en Wodaabe,
one of our very first friends!

just sleep out in the open. If it rains, they get under the mats, under a bush or under the bed. No matter how wet they get they will soon drip dry as the rains come in the heat of 120 degree summer.

We spent a relaxed day, Gundi, Biano and Hima lost in great conversations about the state of the world, trials and tribulations of nomadism and the virtues of 4WD, while Marta, Ann and I gossiped with the women. About 5 o'clock, Shuhlel, Gundi's sister-in-law, announced that she was going out to milk the cattle. This seemed like a good idea to Ann, Marta and me, and with Gundi's permission and Hima's suggestion of a water bottle, we headed off.

By 6 PM we were still walking and had only just reached the outskirts of the herds. According to Shuhlel, the cattle were just "right over there" in the pastureland. Silly us, we should have known what to expect as we already knew what this meant in Wodaabe talk.

As I said before, every Wodaabe and Tuareg nomad from the region was camped out here and the total herd was huge. Gundi's herd, having just arrived that day, was at the far end. I was beginning to get a bit nervous. The sun would be down in an hour and I had no idea how we were going to walk back in the dark. Ann and Marta were no spring chickens, and the terrain was full of little bushes to stumble over, and holes to fall in. We had not thought to bring a flashlight. Shuhlel and her two little girls who had come with us probably had terrific night vision, but we did not.

We made a very odd looking group walking out there into those mammoth herds...three white women of varying ages and shapes, led by one typically tall, thin Wodaabe woman and her two little girls in matching Wodaabe dress, each carrying on their heads empty calabashes for milking. The nomads around us were so surprised to see us that they all came out to greet us. They almost never see white people, and when they do, they are never on foot, and certainly not in the heart of a pastureland. Such quiet gentle folk, these Wodaabe and Tuareg, all walking over shyly to peer at us and shake our hands. These were among the most diffident and reserved, yet welcoming greetings I had ever had.

The dusk was now enveloping us and you can't imagine how remarkably beautiful it was. Everyone and everything in shadow and all the animals doing their dusk time song. Camels, cattle, goats, sheep, were all out there lowing, mooing and bleating, at their lowest decibels, barely audible. It was so peaceful, so primordial that it was biblical. It was so biblical it was holy. And it was so holy I wanted to cry. And, it was magical... animals everywhere and the ghostlike shadows of human beings in flowing robes materializing subtly as they came into view and then fading back into the night as they passed on by. The three of us were totally given over to the ancestral beauty of the sounds, smells and images while pinching ourselves that this was actually real and we truly were out here at this spot at the ends of the earth, so privileged to witness this archaic scene, a living diorama of ages gone by.

But I could only hold this reverie for so long as I would suddenly remember the stark reality. We were out here in the dark, a good hour's walk back to Gundi and the home hearth. Just how I was going to get my two traveling companions back there was beyond me. Why hadn't we thought to take a flashlight? I was convinced that it would never occur to Gundi that we would have a hard time seeing in the dark. Biano would think about it, but where would we be by then? I told myself not to worry. I figured, it was so warm and so balmy, the nomads could lend us blankets or mats, we could sleep on the ground right there and walk back to our camp with Shuhlel and her little girls in the morning. The desert would provide.

Suddenly I saw a tall Wodaabe figure materializing toward me in the dark and a voice said, "Irma, is that REALLY you???" I looked up and recognized Doula, a very entrepreneurial Wodaabe friend of mine from Agadez, where he had a shop of Wodaabe artifacts during the tourist season. But we were currently a good 150 kilometers from Agadez. "Doula," I said, rushing over to take his hand. "Is that really YOU??? What are you doing here?" It seems that, in the off-season, Doula was a nomad out here in this very region, because Doula was a Bii Nga'en Wodaabe and Gundi was his chief. His family was camped in a nearby tent. He had seen whites come in on foot, and since whites never do anything on foot, especially in pasturelands, he came out to see who they were. According to Doula, it could only have been me.

Unknown to Doula, his explanation restored his honor. Every time he had told me in Agadez over the past few years that I had to hurry up and buy something from him because he was leaving in an hour to see his family in the bush, it really was true. And I had thought it was just another Wodaabe line. But in fact, it was the Wodaabe Way. "Doula," I asked. "Any chance you have a flashlight?"

Doula lent us a flashlight, and milking over, we made our way slowly back to our camp, one light serving for all three of us. Sure enough, Gundi met us halfway, having been sent out to find us by Biano. Another 30 minutes and we were back at camp.

Much more than Gundi had been found on this trip.

Wodaabe long horned cattle in the bush. Azouas region, northern Niger.

Biba, one of my oldest and sweetest Wodaabe friends wearing traditional multiple Wodaabe hoop earrings.

CHAPTER TWELVE

"IRMA IS STRONGER THAN THE CAMEL"

Batting 1000 by now in intense Wodaabe experiences, I decided I would next take up the offer of Moneidji Gorsay, that very same chief of the Yamankoe'en Wodaabe I had met at the Gerewol in InGall two summers before in 1990. Moneidji had invited me to come stay with him and his family in the bush, whenever I could. That following November, I was due to take a Reader's Digest crew into the Sahara to shoot a documentary. As we were to do this in Niger, I went a week early so that I could find Moneidji and his family.

I found Moneidji exactly where he said he would be, in the town of Abalak, staying at the home of a Tuareg woman, Madame Aliah. Life is still relatively easy for the Wodaabe in the early winter months, because the water holes are still full from the summer rains, and the children can easily supervise the herds. Later on the waterholes will dry up and the water must be drawn up from deep wells, bucket by bucket for hours on end, until the entire herd is watered. So, November was a time when Moneidji would often come into town to the local market to catch up on the news, staying for a couple of nights at Madame Aliah's. The rest of the family would remain out in the bush, about 15 kilometers away.

I had a vehicle with me so we headed off immediately to join his family whom I had not yet met. We quickly left the asphalted road and barreled into the open bush, with Moneidji navigating in what seemed to be a totally haphazard way. What exactly he was using for landmarks were invisible to me. It all looked like the same nondescript terrain. Here a bush, there a bush. This was his turf though, and one learns never to second-guess a nomad. After an hour of relentless bumping, we were home.

Moneidji Gorsay, a chief of the Yamankoe'en Wodaabe lineage.

Home was at the edge of a narrow and shallow dry river bed and consisted of just the two traditional Wodaabe beds, sitting out there in the landscape, one with its pile of calabashes, and one with a blanket rolled up at one end. Moneidji had three wives and five children. The second wife, Lamin, was out on a trek in the direction of Cameroon.

Wodaabe women are known all over West Africa for their medicinal prowess, herbs and powders and so they often pack up their kits and head out on foot for a few months to sell their wares. They will go in a group of two to three women, maybe one man coming along as well. They just walk along, sleeping out each night on the mat they carry with them. If there is a baby in tow, it is wrapped up in a shawl and toted on the back the way all African women carry their children. If the children are of walking age, they are left at home with the other wives. Lamin had five children and these were all in the camp when we got there.

Young "Bofido" Wodaabe girl in her traditional wrapper and minus any finery.

Didi, Moneidji's third wife, was now "Bofido" and off having her first baby, which according to tradition, she would give birth to at her parent's home, and stay there until the baby was weaned. Once a young woman is married she leaves her familial home and goes to live with her husband's family. When she becomes pregnant with her first child, she then returns to her mother's home where she will stay for the course of the year learning to care for a child and run a Wodaabe home. This state is called "Bofido." Only when her mother deems she has learned all that she needs to know, is she released back into normal daily society. During this time she cannot wear any jewelry or fine clothing. She wears only a plain black wrapper and a simple hairdo. She does not see her husband and cannot look at other men. Usually "Bofidos" graduate to womanhood together with great ceremony and celebration at the annual Worso family reunions.

Two of Lamin's children: her oldest son Bulama and her daughter Hadija.

Tea drinking is as much a habit among the Wodaabe as the Tuareg.

Rhodo, Moneidji's first wife was there taking care of the five kids. I had to learn the name of the first child a bit indirectly, as it is taboo among the Wodaabe for parents to pronounce the name of their first born. Rhodo was able to call Bulama by his name since he was actually Lamin's child, but Moneidji couldn't.

Rhodo and I immediately became fast friends. She spoke better French than Moneidji so communication was much easier. We took my bag out of the truck, which then left to return to Agadez, and I installed myself under the one major shade tree, together with the five kids, Rhodo and Moneidji.

Gradually other Wodaabe came by to say hello. The word was out that Moneidji had a white visitor and you can imagine what a novelty I was. But, saying hello in Wodaabe is not your simple "hi." The greeting, which starts with the traditional "foma, foma," with response of "usay, usay," continues back and forth, and includes questions about the health of the entire family and herds. The greeting is carried out in a very diffident way, following the dictates of the Wodaabe Code of Reserve. Out of respect, Wodaabe

Wodaabe visitor to Moneidji's camp.

men never look at each other during the greeting process.

It was an easy-going afternoon. Nothing to do all day but sit around and say "hello" with the neighbors who came to visit. Supper time and Rhodo brought us a big bowl of millet balls in sauce. Along with the milk from their cows, this is the main staple of the Wodaabe diet, especially in the dry season when the milk supply is more limited. Millet balls come in a great variety. At least three styles that I can attest to...millet porridge in milk in the morning, millet in green sauce during the day, and millet in a kind of Chinese brown sauce in the evening. Important visitors are also honored with the first frothy bowls of milk from their cattle and the slaughtering of a goat or sheep, which is then grilled out over the open fire. I had stopped at the market in town on my way to find Moneidji, and so we had with us a leg of lamb. Upon arrival at camp Moneidji immediately hung it from the thorns of an acacia tree, alongside one that was already festering up there. What with a replacement already in place, he handed its now rank predecessor to Rhodo and told her to cook it up for dinner. So we had quite the feast...millet balls a la Cantonese and spit-grilled lamb shank.

Baby boy Eliasu, second boy Dangana and Rhodo sitting on the family bed.
Note the decoration on the big bed spools made with furniture tacks.

By about 9 o'clock I was getting pretty tired, what with the jet lag and all, and I announced that I would like to go to sleep. Rhodo immediately invited me to sleep over by their bed, but I preferred to sleep in privacy further down the riverbank. Moneidji promptly picked up my bags and the three of us headed down to my chosen spot. It was just above the river bed, on the firm ground of the riverbank. But the Wodaabe often prefer the soft sand of the dry riverbed itself. No sooner did Moneidji plunk my stuff down in the spot I had picked, then he picked it up again and placed it all smack in the middle of the dry riverbed. "No good there," he said. "Much better here!" With a shrug I acquiesced. Quite frankly, I don't really like being in the middle of the riverbed. The ground is all soft and gravely, and the tiny pebbles get into everything. Give me the hard Sealy Posturpedic river bank any day. But, a chief is a chief and I deferred.

Then, I noticed Rhodo. She had a tree branch in her hand and was busy sweeping out the riverbed for me, removing my sleeping area of any twigs, thorns, leaves or whatever. This was no different than if I had straightened up my guest bedroom for her, smoothing out the sheets and fluffing up the pillows on the guest bed. Exactly the same gesture. She was making very sure I would be comfortable for the night. Truly, human beings are the same the world over. But she was doing it in such a primordial context. I mean, how often do you sleep at someone else's home where they sweep out the riverbed for you?

There is something rather mystical about Wodaabe life, which is completely out-of-doors, what with its absence of any live-in structures and space-defining walls. I woke up the next morning in the space I had assumed for my bedroom, but in reality, I was already in the living room. The mere act of opening and closing doors and moving from one defined space into another, provides us "indoor types" with a moment of psychological transition that we are not ever aware of, until we notice its absence. But here, in the open turf of the Wodaabe, there are no such transitions. As there are no walls in Wodaabeland and all activity at the home takes place in the same basic spot, you are always already arrived at where you were going. This may sound a bit like an Alice in Wonderland conundrum, but I was truly struck by the absence of these moments. Perhaps it's a statement of how so intensely preoccupied we are with where we are, that moving on actually requires a measure of transitional time. But how quickly we adjust. Within two days I had easily adapted to the Wodaabe parameters of time and space. The absence of transition and the simplicity of already being there were wonderful.

The next day Rhodo and I went to a recently rain-filled waterhole to get water. This meant loading two huge plastic 20 gallon jerry cans (one of the few Wodaabe admissions to modern life) on to one of the donkeys, and the two of us onto the other donkey. The baby donkey, which would follow along no matter what, was ridden by Dangana, Moneidji's six year old son. The donkey of choice or, more accurately, of availability in this part of the world, is actually the same donkey that in Ethiopia is called the Abyssinian Ass. Sweet little grey-colored beasts with the mark of the cross on their backs. This is the same donkey Mary rode on her trip to Bethlehem. Hence, according to legend, the cross. Donkeys are great beasts of burden and certainly here, carry their weight in water.

30 minutes later we arrived at the pond. This had to have been one of the more uncomfortable animal rides I have ever had. Not that roller coasters, go-carts or Ferris wheels turn me on either. The best place to sit on the donkey is back on his haunches,

i.e., the rear seat, because that is where there is the most padding. (Quite contrary to the camel. If anyone ever offers you the back seat of the camel, you'd do best to walk.) Rhodo was in the rear, as hostess, and I was given the front as best viewing position. But the donkey's spine up front is about as sharp and narrow as it can be and this is hardly comfortable for man, woman or child. Except, apparently, for Dangana, (the little show-off) who rode his baby donkey lounging every which way he felt like across the animal's back.

We unloaded the jerry cans and Rhodo dragged them into the middle of this temporary natural pond. This didn't look much like water I even wanted to walk in, let alone drink. Every cow and his uncle was there as well, drinking, munching and pooping. Exactly the kind of water the CDC, and any book on how to enjoy the outdoor life, tells you to avoid. I did. Rhodo filled the jerry cans with the help of the calabash she had worn upside down on her head as a sun helmet on the ride over. 20 gallon jerry cans take a painstakingly long time to fill when you are using a one-quart aluminum bowl. And she was careful to filter the water as best she could, letting any sediment settle before she made each scoop. The Wodaabe like these natural pools that fill up underneath groves of trees when the rains come because they believe that the nutrients from the trees fall down into the water. I would be hard pressed to convince Rhodo that this wasn't good water. And, there wasn't a long list of alternatives to offer.

With Dangana helping we were ready to leave about an hour later. We loaded up the now full jerry cans onto the two adult donkeys and Dangana hopped on his baby donkey. Rhodo climbed up on one of the donkeys, but I declined to ride. Walking seemed a much more comfortable idea.

The steering mechanism on a donkey is quite simple. You use a stick and tap him against the left side of his neck if you want to go right, and against the right side if you want to go left. This usually works, but somehow the straight-ahead mechanism got left out of the design. Stopping is another problem still on the drawing board. For the moment, the temporary solution that works best is just to yank hard while simultaneously pulling back, on the donkey's mane.

Dangana challenged me to a race back to camp. He would race his baby donkey and I would do my New York speed walk, which movement he found exceedingly silly. Not difficult to understand why. Wodaabe walk as a way of life, never a sport. The Wodaabe walk is tall, straight and elegant. A glide across the landscape. Tuareg walk the same way. Because the Wodaabe, being cattle herders, "walk for a living," it would never occur to them to make a game out of it. Kind of like bringing coals to Newcastle or the proverbial busman's holiday. The exaggerated movements of speed walking could only produce hysterics.

The race started out with me easily assuming the straight ahead position. Dangana gave his baby a swift kick and he too achieved the same direction. There we were, neck and neck, with the donkey pushing ahead. But something to the left caught the baby's eye, and suddenly Dangana was swerving off to that side. Just about cut right in front of me. I would have called "foul," but Dangana was, after all, only six years old. Dangana gave the baby a good bang on the side of the neck to get him to reverse direction. So, naturally what did the baby do now but head in just the opposite direction. I, meanwhile, was happily speeding forward, as true to my path as the cartoon Roadrunner. A few more figure eights and the baby donkey realized that he was going nowhere, and his mother, with Rhodo on top of her, was getting farther away. The baby let out a panicked haw and then took off like a shot to catch up, but I had well outdistanced Rhodo and her steed, who really wasn't in any great hurry, given the weight of that jerry can. Dangana continued to figure-eight his way back to camp.

Need I say who won the race that day? The word was out that night: Irma was stronger than a camel. Believe me, that would not have been the compliment of my choice, but neither is the camel my locomotion of choice. So, I simply took the compliment for all that it was worth, and settled in once again comfortably to my bed in the riverbed.

The truck came to pick me up two days later to begin the Reader's Digest documentary and I left, promising to return a few months later in February, 1992. I knew I would be back in Niger then with a group of Turtle Tours travelers for a Niger Sahara Desert expedition. But by February, the Tuareg rebellion had broken out and it was unsafe to go deep into Moneidji's part of the bush, what with skirmishes between the Tuareg rebels and the Niger military. **Little did I expect that I would not be able to return until 1994!**

Rhodo and I sitting together at her home in the bush while she puts the finishing touches on the Elletel she is making for me.

My dear friend Rhodo, after whom I named my dog. Once I did this, Rhodo and her husband Chief Moneidji named one of their cows after me.

CHAPTER THIRTEEN

AMONG THE HAMAR IN ETHIOPIA'S OMO VALLEY: BLESSINGS AND BABIES

My searches for more and more remote tribal peoples took me eventually to Southern Ethiopia's Omo Valley, homeland to ritual decoration at its finest. Some of the world's most ritualistically imprinted and greatest looking people are to be found there and I knew I would be like the kid in the proverbial candy store.

I made my first visit with six clients in tow in 1990. The action started the moment I boarded the plane in Frankfurt for our 10 hour flight to Addis Ababa. Dressed rather exotically as usual in my traditional baggy Saharan pants and wearing lots of silver jewelry and amulets, I stood out from almost everyone on the plane. Other than my group of Turtle Tours travelers who were accompanying me there wasn't a single other "traveler." Everyone else, with no exception, was some form of Aid Worker…either working for a government organization or an 'N.G.O." non-governmental organization. They were all in street clothes or business suits looking very practical and ready to dive into their work. We, however, looked like we were ready for adventure and that seemed more appealing to many on the plane.

As I walked down the aisle to my seat, a very handsome man grabbed my arm and stopped me as I was passing him. "Who are you and why are you going to Ethiopia?" he demanded of me. Most intrigued by his attention, I explained that I was the owner and director of an American Adventure Travel Company, Turtle Tours, specializing in remote tribal peoples and that I was on my way to the Omo Valley with six clients to meet and learn about several of the most fascinating tribes in the world and their cultures…in particular the Hamar, Karo, Mursi, Bume, Bodi and the Borana. "Very ambitious!" he said. "I know!" I responded, smiling brightly.

He lit up and introduced himself as Ivo Strecker, the one anthropologist who had been working among the Hamar for 20 years. He was a professor of anthropology, spending half the year in Ethiopia including teaching at the University of Addis Ababa and doing his research while living among the Hamar, and the other half in his native Germany teaching there. He took an immediate liking to me and offered to introduce me and my group to his Hamar family down in the Omo. This particular family was that of Chief Aikey Barimas, one of several Hamar chiefs. They lived at a site called Dambaite, in the Turmi region of Hamar territory. Bingo! We had hit pay dirt before the plane had even left the tarmac in Frankfurt.

What a gift this was. Although there were several different tribal groups down in the Omo, there usually was only one anthropologist researching each group, so to meet on the plane the one and only anthropologist to have been working with the Hamar for 20 years and have him introduce us to his "family" was an incredible opportunity.   As Ivo was busy teaching at the University, he introduced me and my group via a letter written by him to them in phonetic Hamar which he gave me to read to the chief, presenting myself and my group to him and his retinue.

Armed with Ivo's letter and instructions to stop at a market in the south to buy a 50 pound bag of coffee chaff to give to the chief and his family, we headed out early the next day. Three days of driving from Addis and we finally reached Hamar territory, deep in the Omo Valley. We couldn't have hoped for a better entree into a local tribal community.   We stopped in the miniscule Hamar town of Turmi for sodas and instructions to Chief Aikey's compound at Dambaite, and then we continued on.

Three Hamar girlfriends Turmi, Hamar territory, Omo Valley, Ethiopia.

In the meanwhile, I had already fallen in love with the Hamar at very first glance. Just seeing them walking along the road was enough to win me over. Hamar women are very beautiful... usually very fine featured with rich red brown skin. They are also ritually decorated to the hilt. They all wear wrap-around skirts of goat skins embellished with
 beads, metal zippers...whatever they can find. They cover their breasts with a goat skin bib decorated with cowrie shells and beads. An ancient form of currency, cowries were to

Africans what gold was to other cultures. Up and down their arms and legs they wear a host of aluminum bracelets, kneelets and anklets. Depending on their age, their hair is worn from very short to shoulder length for adult women and would drive most hair stylists wild with envy. If you can imagine long strands of pop-it beads covered with red ochre and animal fat, you can envision the typical Hamar hairstyle. A short pop-it head fringe in the front and longer pop-its in the back. Why it doesn't turn into one mess of mush when they sleep I'll never know, but it just doesn't. Even first thing in the morning, these woman look great.

  On top of all this, they wear lots of metal jewelry, most of which is there to clue you in on their marital status. If they are young and unmarried, they wear a kind of aluminum duck bill in their hair. If they are married, they wear two to three heavy metal bands around their necks, the first two given to them by the male members of their family. The third can only be worn under two conditions: the woman must be the first wife of her husband and she must have given birth to a boy. Sure simplifies things for the Hamar men who might be out cruising at the weekly local market.

Our friend Eree, from Turmi region, Hamar territory, Omo Valley, Ethiopia.

Married woman wearing the "esente," the necklace with the phallic protrusion that indicates she is the first wife of her husband and has given birth to a boy.

Hamar styles for all ages and all occasions.

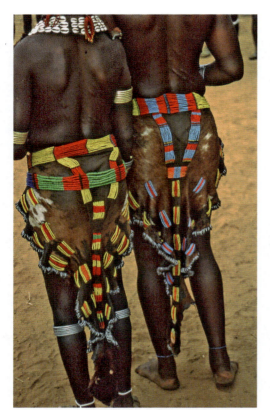

Young Hamar women in line performing a traditional Hamar dance. Dambaite, Turmi region, southern Ethiopia.

*Boys and girls dance with each other. The girls rub their aluminum bracelets
together to make music for the dance.*

The men aren't so bad to look at either. They aren't as ornamented, but if they have managed to kill an enemy or a ferocious animal, they wear their hair done up in a multicolored painted clay bun at the back, into which they can stick all manner of things, from ostrich feathers to safety pins. This hairdo, though, is not specific to Hamar men. Men from the neighboring Karo, Bume and Galeb tribes in Ethiopia also wear it, as do the Turkana in Kenya. I think of them as "warrior buns." The edges of their ears are lined with furniture tack-like earrings.

Karo man with clay hair bun indicating he has killed an enemy or a ferocious beast. He is also wearing a lip plug in his lower lip.

All the men wear a very short, wrapped cloth around their buttocks, which always manages to fall exactly one centimeter below their privates. They must have one remarkable tailor. This mini-wrap is held up by a WW II cartridge belt, and the final ornamentation is the individual's weapon of choice, which ranges from a tall spear, to an old WW II vintage Italian rifle, to an AK-47, their only concession to the modern world.

And when they are really in the mood, like cruising at the aforementioned weekly markets, they paint their legs and body with a chalky ash into which they draw designs. This time it's the Bloomingdale's leggings buyer who is wild with envy. Finally, without exception, they all walk around carrying the world's tiniest stool, actually a headrest, which doubles as a pillow at night and the smallest possible portable seat during the day. A man is never without his headrest as he uses it day and night. Not a bad looking group of people to have fallen upon so easily.

Hamar men displaying the art of body painting.

Hamar man with feather adornment in his hair. The red stripe across his forehead indicates that he has killed someone or something ferocious.
In addition to many beads, he is also wearing a metal watch strap as adornment hanging from his neck. These are a very popular decoration in the Omo Valley region.

Hamar man with scarification on his chest. These are like notches on a gun belt. They indicate that the man has killed an enemy or a ferocious animal. The scarification is done by making small slits in the skin with a knife and then rubbing ashes or a pebble into the wound. As the cuts heal, the ash or the pebble causes the skin to form a bump.

Murso, a Hamar Elder from the Turmi region, is highly skilled in Divination.

We arrived at Dambaite about 40 minutes later and drove into the compound honking our horns. The main compound had one big Hamar oval shaped, domed and thatched hut and one smaller round one. Scattered around the outside of this compound, which was all enclosed within a very irregular log fence, were several other smaller huts for other members of the extended family, including the chief's brothers and sisters, sons, daughters and their spouses and a bunch of grandchildren. Outside the far side of the compound was a large corral into which were led all the family's cattle and goats each night for security after their daily grazing outside in the nearby scrub brush.

The Elders of the Barimas family at Dambaite. The man holding my hand is Chief Aikey Barimas. The other man is Alma Barimas, Chief Aikey's brother and father of Shada. Absent is Aikey's brother-in-law Ailoo.
We are sitting outside Aikey's hut where Ivo Strecker has lived for many years while doing his anthropological research on the Hamar.

It was late in the afternoon so most of the family were there, including Chief Aikey who emerged from the big hut through the tiniest peephole of a doorway possible to greet us. Hamar huts are built for defense so entry into them is made quite difficult in case the person desiring entry is not a visitor but an intruder. Within minutes all the other huts had emptied out and every family member including the children had run over to greet us. Yohannes, my tour guide from Addis, explained our purpose and our letter from Ivo. Everyone was so wonderfully friendly and so glad to hear news from Ivo that they kept shaking our hands and pumping our arms in enthusiasm! Cowhide mats were quickly pulled out through the peephole door and arranged for us to sit on. We were quite pleased with ourselves as privileged guests in such a household.

Sassy Aikey, Chief Aikey's son. Dambaite family compound.
Hamar territory, southern Ethiopia.

Barinda, another member of the Barimas extended family at Dambaite, with her children and their friends.

Younger members of the Barimas extended family at Dambaite.

The first thing I did was read the letter in phonetic Hamar to everyone. Ivo had written it very carefully so that even though I had no clue at all what it said, all the Hamar did. He sent greetings to everyone, asked about everyone's health including that of the cows, and said that he and his family were well. It also explained that we were new American friends of Ivo and that we had brought Chief Aikey a big sack of coffee chaff as a gift. Ivo also asked the chief to serve us coffee if we had time.

We apparently made the chief's day by showing up like this and to honor us, he asked Kari, Sassy Aikey's wife, to serve us coffee in the traditional way. But this was no coffee service as we know it. What we were drinking was actually a thin brownish liquid made not from the beans but from the coffee chaff. And we were drinking it out of their best demitasse cups, huge gourds maybe 15 inches in diameter, that had been cut in half for the purpose.

Traditional Hamar coffee service, made by boiling the chaff of the coffee bean.

I noticed that Kari had a mess of scars across her back. These were not the intricate carefully incised scars of "cicatrization," whose objective is to render the body more beautiful and sensual through elaborate decoration. No indeed. These looked like whip lashes that had been rendered with no thought whatsoever to esthetics. I casually asked the chief what happened. Maybe I misinterpreted and she fell into a fire or something? Nope, no fire.

Hamar woman with two kinds of body scarification, both intentional.
On her upper left shoulder are three rows of raised scars made by rubbing ash or
a pebble into each slit made in the skin. On her lower back are scars created by
whip lashings she has received at Maz Bull Jumping Coming of Age ceremonies.

It seems she had received these lashes during a ceremony called the "Bullah" or "Jumping of the Bulls." This is a rite of passage that a boy goes through when he is about to gain his manhood and become engaged to be married. He must run back and forth four times across the backs of many cows all lined up in a row for the purpose, without falling down. While he is busy running, his sisters and female cousins are ritually whipped as a sign of their enthusiasm and devotion. Those girls who have been whipped display their wounds very proudly. His run successfully completed, he is allowed to join the "Maz" or next age set, and his engagement is officially announced. If he does fall, he is shamed before the many guests who have been invited to witness his coming of age. The ceremony also includes offering a feast of home made beer and sorghum porridge to all the guests, speeches made on his behalf by friends and, of course, Grandma getting her hair redone for the occasion.

Our young friend Naitey, completing his run across the backs of several cows.

I can't help but think that our Jewish Bar Mitzvah boys are getting off a bit too easy in this coming of age stuff, but I'll not press the issue because at age 13 they are much too young to be married.

I noticed also that most of the women and men at Dambaite had had their lower incisor teeth removed. I found this curious as the Hamar are of Omotic origin (originally from the Omo Valley region), while the custom of removing these teeth is generally practiced only by various tribes of Nilotic origin (coming from the Nile basin). I must have been in my typical questioning mood because I asked the chief about this also. He explained that no, it is not a typical Hamar custom, however, many years ago they went to live among the neighboring Galeb tribe for security reasons. The Galeb being Nilotic, were quite horrified that their Hamar house guests were all running around with all their teeth intact. From their point of view, only donkeys have a full set of teeth. Thoroughly embarrassed by this comparison, being very polite and wishing to accommodate their hosts, this group of Hamar tactfully removed their lower front teeth as well.

Grandmas's hairdo is getting a touch-up. A combination of red ocher powder obtained from rocks in the nearby mountains and butter is rubbed into it.

We had a great first visit and Chief Aikey made me promise to come back and visit again on my next trip back to Ethiopia. Then it was time to say goodbye to our new friends and continue on our journey to meet the rest of the tribes who were on our list, including the Karo, Mursi, Bode, Bume and the Borana. As Ivo had noted that fateful day in the plane from Frankfurt to Addis, it was indeed a very ambitious list. We had a lot of people to meet and ground to cover. It was time for "Wagons Ho!"

Political problems kept me out of Ethiopia for the two years following my first visit in 1990. When I finally went back in January,1993 to the Omo region with a group of clients, I took everyone to Turmi to find Chief Aikey, my Hamar friend. I was the one "found" first, down at the weekly Hamar market. Long arms suddenly wrapped around me from behind and whirled me into the smiling faces and bear hugs of Sassy Aikey and Shada, chief Aikey's son and son in law whom I had met at our first visit in 1990. All this was much to the astonishment of all the other local tribespeople. The only whites they were used to seeing were missionaries and I suspect that I didn't look much like one. We rounded up my clients who were dispersed throughout the market and went off to visit the chief. The welcome was just as warm and the coffee just as good and I promised to come back again the following November. By now the chief seemed to have adopted me. No doubt he liked the bags of coffee and salt I always brought with me as house gifts for him and his family. Or, maybe he too just liked my jewelry.

When I returned once again in November, 1993 Chief Aikey was waiting for me. We had our usual visit with traditional coffee for the group and the whole family was there for the encounter. When we were ready to leave, the chief announced that his new third wife was pregnant and that the baby would be due in a few months. I should mention that the chief was about 60 years old, and his third wife, Ali, was about 20. If the baby were a girl, he said he would name it after me, "Ilma." "Irma" was somehow very difficult for Aikey to pronouce and all the family members followed suit. Or maybe it was just something cultural.

The Hamar elders reading the intestines of a goat to get answers to questions of importance for an individual or a group.

It happens that the Hamar are quite good at the art of Divination or Augury. They make a habit of reading the entrails of certain animals to determine the answer to something in the future, foretelling issues like weather conditions for travel, possible wars, how a new born baby's life will unfold, and occasionally the outcomes of presidential elections...the latter usually for me and my groups, but only in election years. There are only a few elders who have this special talent or ability of divination.

I found myself wondering why Chief Aikey didin't call in the elders right away so I at least would know in advance if I needed to bring anything special... a new dress for me, 200 pounds of coffee chaff for him... hmm...considering that this child would be my godchild, possibly even the most up-to-date version of the Encyclopedia Britannica. There's an idea! Now that I think of it, though, there hasn't been anyone at the front door lately selling it.

 Language is often a telling reflection of a culture. The Hamar are agro-pastoralists with large herds of cattle and small fields of sorghum, a grain that is very common to East Africa and grows on a tall stalk. Like other East African cattle herders, they have over 25 words in their language that relate to this beast. The Mursi tribe, who also live in the south Omo region, are cattle herders as well. They define all their colors in terms of cattle. If you show a Mursi a color he has never seen, like purple, he will most likely respond, "there is no such animal." Want to know what happens when you study our language? You discover that we have over 50 words that relate to time. Not very difficult to figure out what we should intuit from that.

Ethiopia was by now becoming one of my three top destinations, the other two being Niger and Mali, and In March, 1994 I was back once again in Ethiopia with yet another group. First on my agenda was to find out the status of the baby's birth, so on arrival in Hamar territory we immediately went looking for the chief. He was by now a big honcho, as chief of the region, and wasn't at the family homestead at Dambaite when we arrived. But my special friend Barinda was there. Barinda informed us that the baby girl had indeed been born, but that she and her mother were all the way down at the river with the herds. This certainly wouldn't make for easy viewing of this apparent goddaughter of mine.

So, after our usual round of ceremonial coffee chaff in Barinda's best set of 15 inch demitasse gourd cups, we climbed back into our vehicles and headed into town in search of the chief. We parked at the local bar, and suddenly there was Aikey, waving his arms madly and shouting "Ilma, Ilma," running over to me and catching me up in another one of those huge Hamar hugs. He couldn't stop shouting out his incredulity that the baby had just been born and there I was. In point of fact, once we actually saw baby Ilma, we realized that she had been born about six weeks ago, but we took into account that the Hamar don't have the same profoundly developed sense of time that we do. Theirs is instead a much more highly developed sense of cattle. To each, his own.

Naturally, given the occasion, I invited everyone into the bar for a drink. The chief and I shared a bottle of "tej," the oldest alcoholic drink in the world. This is Ethiopian honey wine, or what the ancients referred to as mead, made from honey fermented with hops. In his growing and bubbling enthusiasm, the chief began to bless me repeatedly in the traditional

Hamar way. "Pshshshsh," he went, kind of spitting and spraying the sound into the air with a sweeping motion of his head. "Pshshshshshsh," another time with a mouthful of tej. Not being a Christian, I have had little experience with anointment by holy water, however, caught up in the spirit of the moment, I really didn't mind. I am fond of tej, regardless of the form.

I actually had experienced this kind of blessing four years ago on that very first trip to Ethiopia in 1990. After meeting and visiting with Aikey and family, we headed overland to find the Karo tribe, who are related to the Hamar in language and customs. Once there my group and I went down to the Omo River to bathe. Also bathing was a Karo man with a truly magnificent body. All muscular ripples wrapped in a deep red brown color skin. This great looking gentleman had laid down his AK-47 rifle, which all Karo men carry as a modern means of protection from an ancient tribal rivalry, removed his cartridge belt and his perfectly tailored mini-wrap and was bathing "starkers." Quite frankly, it was hard for the feminine contingent in my group to keep our eyes off this extraordinary display of masculine beauty, so we simply plopped down on the river bank closest to him and settled in to watch. Eventually the men in our group finished bathing, and went back to camp, not a little disgruntled by the extent of our attentions elsewhere.

Karo men all with their "warrior" hairbuns. Karo men look and act tougher looking than Hamar men, but they have to be to survive in their particular environment.

163

The Karo tribe are essentially an endangered species as there are less than 2,000 Karo left. They live in three villages alongside the Omo River in huts with doorways even smaller and more dificult to access than the Hamar doorways. The reason for this super small, down on your knees, and then crawl in on your belly ingress is that the Bume tribe, a larger and very aggressive group that lives on the other side of the Omo River from the Karo, was always threatening to cross over the Omo and annihilate the entire group, men, women and children included. Consequently, the Karo often sported a similar "bad guy" attitude, doing a lot of "tough guy" posturing themselves. Our Karo bather, not having extended any kind of friendly "hello ladies, why don't you come join me in this delightful (croc infested) water" welcome seemed like he might also be familiar with this type of posturing, but we didn't let it bother us.

We remained steadfastly and staunchly glued to the subject at hand. Noticing our warm glazed smiles whenever he looked back at his audience, he asked if he could borrow a bar of soap to wash his miniskirt. Of course. And wash, he did. Over and over again. Afterall, a bar of soap didn't come his way that often. When he finally finished, he walked back to us, handed us the soap with a slightly visible nod of thanks, no smile, not even one weeny one for the blissed out women sitting on the river bank...just a brusque nod.

And then, suddenly, taking us fully by surprise, he stood very straight and tall, took a very deep breath and "pshshshshshed" into the air over all of us with a wide sweeping motion of his head. As Aikey had not yet blessed us the day before at our first meeting, we didn't yet know or understand the gesture. And, truth to tell, it can have a most disconcerting effect when you don't know what it's all about, especially when it rolls out of the mouth of a "warrior bun" wearing, AK-47 toting, "starkers" nude male emerging from a crocodile infested river right in front of you. But, as we all lived to tell about it, we guessed it must be okay. Back in Addis eight days later, Ivo, the anthropologist, explained the meaning of this rather startling display over a bar of soap. Our squeaky clean Mr. Karo was thanking us for our kindness by blessing us in the traditional way of his people. This apparently was one of the traditions that the Hamar and the Karo share.

As a quick point of interest, the only two tribes among the several tribes, notably the Hamar, Karo, Mursi, Bume, Bodi and Galeb, who live down in the Omo and intermarry are the Hamar and the Karo. All the rest are enemies. How did this happen? Simple! First, they are all agro-pastoralists, meaning that they all are cattle herders as well as farmers. Add to this the fact that they live in a wild west territory that is very difficult to police due to so much tall brush in which to hide cattle, this makes it very easy for them to become cattle rustlers. Would you develop a fondness for people who kept stealing your cattle? And really, would you want your daughter or your son to marry one of them??? So, there you have it...the perfect recipe for putting a potentially friendly neighbor on your enemy list!

My apologies for the many digressions from the story at hand...the naming of little Irma. Often there pops up a wonderfully exotic or unusual tidbit about a particular tribe that I just have to share with you, or bite my tongue while I try to stay on topic. To me, these constitute an often important part of the tapestry of their culture and what makes them so fascinating to us, in addition to their way of dress. I would feel remiss if I didn't include them...no matter where they butt into the conversation.

So, getting back to the scene in the bar in Turmi where the chief and I continued to drink tej to the birth of Ilma, punctuated by the now very familiar and occasionally wet "pshshshshes...." the rest of the group was seated comfortably against the wall, drinking their beers and enjoying being out of the sun. Thelma, one of my favorite trip members, got up to go out for a walk, so I called her over to be introduced to the chief.

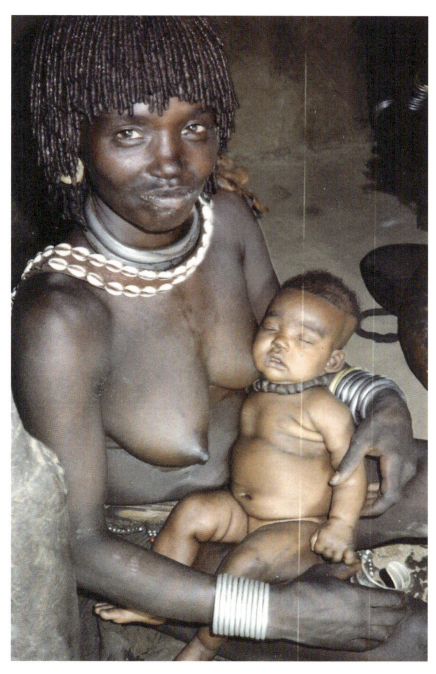

Ali holding her six week old little baby Irma/Ilma.

Enthusiastically, she walked right up to him to offer her hand, and received the brunt of a long tej-filled blessing, full in the face. Her sunglasses now needed windshield wipers. Her head flew back in total surprise, not having expected anything of the sort. She regained her composure, gave me a most sidewards, quizzical glance and continued to shake his hand. Tej was also dripping from the edges of her sunhat, but polite to the end, she paid it no mind. When the chief finally released her, she dashed outside and I could see her, well out of the chief's view, quickly grabbing a Kleenex and "kleening" off. Now I blessed myself for always surrounding myself with trooper travelers like Thelma. The rest of my group was witness to this entire little scene and was now distinctly hugging the walls where they were sitting. At least for that moment, there was nothing in the world that would motivate them to get up. Introductions to Aikey, albeit a Chief of the Hamar, could wait til later.

The chief now announced to me and Yohannes, my guide who had become an integral part of every tour and as much a member of the family as me, that we must have an official naming ceremony for the baby, and that he would dispatch his son Saissy Aikey down to the river to bring Ali and Ilma back. We agreed that the ceremony would be the next morning. I was very flattered as I realized the importance of this ceremony for the chief and his family. It was all up to me now.

That evening I discussed the ceremony with my group. We decided that if I were going to take this seriously, I would have to do it in my own tradition. The baby would have a Jewish naming ceremony and she would be given a Jewish name. Carol, also Jewish, helped me work out a ceremony and the prayers we would recite. (Back home I suppose it's the rabbi who takes care of all these details.) The next morning all 12 of us, including my 10 clients plus my guide Yohannes and I, arrived at the chief's house and were ushered in with great ceremony.

The Chief's house was also the house where Ivo lived when he was down there doing his research. It was an "almost" typical Hamar structure, a round domed hut built out of bent sticks and covered with layers of thatch; the only untypical part being that it was oval and had two rooms. The second room had been added on to accommodate Ivo, his work and occasionally Ivo's family. This two-room affair was quite large and very sturdy with huge central supports, but it also had the typical killer tiny doorways with a knee-high sill, that seemed to be made only for Hamar bodies and flexibility. Not very easy for attackers to enter as well as a gymnastic feat worthy of at least a silver medal for us Westerners to climb through, as we had to bend in half to get in while bringing our knees up to our chins. Certainly not our usual posture when making an entrance. Interior decoration was at a minimum, but with no windows, you couldn't see much anyway…just the usual gourd containers for milking and water, the usual calabashes for eating and drinking, and some animal skins for sitting and sleeping on. Beyond that, the Hamar don't have or need much else.

The whole family was there seated on the floor of the oval room with Ali and baby Ilma in the center. All the women were in their ritual best. Pop-it bead and ochre-greased hairdos, skin bibs and skirts decorated with beads and cowries, aluminum bracelets and anklets. Sassy Aikey had chalked his body white for the occasion and had an ornamental feather in his hairbun. We took our places, seated on the ground in a semi-circle on the animal skins that had been placed there for us. I had already told Yohannes that he was to translate everything exactly as I said it, because it came from my tradition and it was very important to me that the chief understand it all.

I sat down and was handed the baby and told to kiss her, or so I thought. Apparently I had misunderstood. "No, no" said Yohannes. I was to lick the baby, not kiss it. I licked baby Ilma as best I could, valiantly trying to follow instructions. After all, licking babies is not part of any ritual I have grown up with, and then I handed her back to Ali.

I survived the licking and continued on with the baby naming ceremony.

The chief offered the first blessing. **"Pshshshshshsh."** Now it was indeed my turn to take over the ceremony. I took out my traveling Sabbath tea candles which I had in reserve for the following Friday eve. I began by explaining that, in the Jewish tradition, candles are a symbol of light and hope. The chief **"pshshshshshshed"** in the background. I lit the candles. Another **"pshshshshsh."** I then explained that all Jewish children have a Jewish name and this baby's name was now **"Irma Rebecca."**

"Ilma Abaca," the chief smiled, repeated and blessed, **"Pshshshshsh."**

"Irma Rebecca," Yohannes stated precisely and more firmly.

"Ilma Abaca," the chief repeated once more with great enthusiasm and another long **"pshshshsh"** for the group.

Yohannes looked helplessly at me, as there was no way the chief was going to get the r's right. At my signal, he acquiesed. Afterall, it is really the essence and not the form that matters. The chief smiled contentedly. Next, I explained that we give thanks in a prayer for the baby. I recited my amended Sabbath "brucha," choking up on the words as I always do whenever anything moves me. Carol was at my side, rubbing my back, helping me to get the Hebrew words out. The chief continued to punctuate with blessings, **"pshshshshsh, pshshshshshsh."** My blessing ended literally in thanks, not for the Sabbath, but for the beautiful baby, Ilma Abaca.

In response, the chief now addressed us. He pointed to the central supports of his tribal home in which we were sitting. "These posts," he said, "support this home, the way our American friends stand by us and this baby."

I picked up where I had left off and told him that it was also part of our tradition to give gifts to the parents for having brought the child into the world, and to the child for gracing us with the joy of her presence. I handed a bracelet to Ali, and a fancy shirt to the chief, complete with epaulets. Afterall, he was a chief and now preferred western clothing for government meetings. Both presents had been given to me that very morning by Helen, one of the members of the group. Helen is the kind of traveler who is prepared for all eventualities. We included a bar of soap with the shirt. The shirt would certainly have to be kept clean and as already noted, I'd had previous good experiences with soap.

Next, I took out a stack of one hundred one bihr notes, the equivalent of about 20 dollars, but a considerable amount of money to the average Hamar, even if he were a chief. I explained that this money was to help feed the baby and keep her healthy for a long life.

More "pshshshshshshes" from the chief and then he began to speak, Yohannes as always translating. "Money is like the dew," he said. "Oh dear," I thought, and was suddenly fearful that he would say "do you really expect this little amount of money to take care of a baby's lifetime?"   Didn't I know about inflation! But no. He continued, his blessings by now more extensive and group-inclusive.

"Money," he said, "money is like the wind. It comes and goes. But a name, this name, Ilma Abaca, will last forever." I wasn't the only teary-eyed one in the group.

We finished the naming ceremony with coffee in the traditional coffee gourds, which was being served by Hailanda, the chief's sister-in-law, sitting near me. When I had finished my coffee, the chief told me to pick out a gourd to keep as a remembrance of this occasion. I picked the one nearest me. Suddenly a squabble ensued between the chief and Hailanda. It seemed that I had picked out the best one and was breaking up her good Sunday set. The squabble continued, so I put it back down. It was soon all resolved when she took back the one I had chosen and handed me, with a reassuring satisfied smile, the one of her choice. This one had been broken and repaired in the traditional native way and was probably the very one I would have picked out, if I had taken more time. We were all content. I was given the baby to lick one more time and the ceremony was over. **Ilma Abaca was now my official goddaughter.**

A few minutes later, when we were back at our vehicles in the midst of hugs and goodbyes, Sassy Aikey, the chief's son, rushed over to present me with his best, well oiled and patined headrest and Barinda came running over to present me with her best demitasse coffee gourd. On my next trip to Ethiopia the following August when visiting with Aikey again, I found those very same Sabbath tea candles that I used in the naming ceremony carefully preserved on Aikey's shelf next to all his best and most special objects inside the hut.

Sadly, both Chief Aikey and baby Ilma Abaca died a year later in 1995.

I continued bringing Turtle Tours travelers to Ethiopia, sometimes twice yearly. However, instead of staying in the local campground in Turmi for two nights while visiting with the Hamar, at the family's invitation we decamped and began setting up our private camp right inside the Dambaite compound next to the chief's hut.

It was perfect. The family members would come and visit with us in the evenings. The neighborhood girls would get together and put on a dance which we gladly joined. We had coffee ceremonies each morning with blessings by the chief's brother Alma and brother-in-law Ailoo before heading out on our day's adventure.

Eventually I moved the TurtleWill Mobile Medical Clinic Hamar site to Dambaite from where it had been in Turmi. Turmi actually had a real clinic of its own and changing our clinic to Dambaite meant we would be reaching many more people truly without access to medical care. Each member of the family was very proud to be able to host such a service for all the people in the region of Dambaite. This Mobile Clinic Program ran through 2010.

I was unable to return to Ethiopia in 2003 and 2004, but was able to return in 2005 with the TurtleWill Mobile Clinic. There was a wonderful surprise waiting for me. Three of the families had had babies in 2003. They were all baby girls, and they were all named Irma, I mean "Ilma." The happy couples were Sassy (Aikey's son) and Kari; Shada (Aikey's nephew, son of Aikey's brother Alma) and Aila (Barinda's son)) and Warka. On arrival at Dambaite I was promptly whirled up once again into huge Hamar bear hugs, told the exciting news of the births and that I needed to officially name each of the girls as I had done 11 years before in 1994, giving them each a Jewish name to tack on to "Ilma." And no, I didn't have to lick them. They were now too big.

We had the ceremony the following morning, early before the patients began to arrive and line up at the corner of the compound where we had installed the medical tent.

Ilma Leah, Ilma Raycha and Ilma Sarah with me at Dambaite, 2005.

Added to the family tree were now:

  Ilma Sarah, daughter of Sassy and Kari
  Ilma Rachel, pronounced Raycha, daughter of Shada and Goitee
  Ilma Leah, daughter of Aila and Warka

What a wonderful tradition that Aikey started and what a very touching legacy for me!

The three "Ilmas" with their paper dolls, Dambaite,

CHAPTER FOURTEEN

THE HIMBA NOMADS OF NAMIBIA: "THOSE MEN IN THE RADIO"

The Himba are one of Africa's least disturbed and most traditional tribes of nomadic cattle herders. I had wanted to visit the Himba of the Kaokoveld in northern Namibia for many years, but the war with South Africa prevented anyone from going up there. As long as Namibia, which was then called South West Africa, was at war with South Africa, the Himba, who had "claimed migratory residence" in the very north of their country, almost at the border of Angola, remained isolated. Now that the war was over, we were able to go, and so we did in April, 1995.

Our new Himba lady friends at their cattle camp:
Moogahunya, Karentu, Magaheyga and Mautungwavee.

What we found was a still very traditional group of cattle herders roaming the wilds of the Kaokoveld. The women, beautiful indeed, were completely decorated from head to toe. They wore jewelry made out of metals, rabbit fur and shells and had bonnets of goat fur on their heads. They were bare breasted while around their bottoms they wore an unusual array of animal skins charmingly fashioned to look like ruffles. They coated their bodies and hairdos thoroughly with hematite powder mixed with animal fat, giving their skins a rich deep red color. This "cosmetic" is used as much for esthetics as it is to protect their skins from the sun. It also has a certain magical and religious quality of purification, and is used particularly in marriage ceremonies when young girls must give up their own religious taboos and adopt those of their husbands.

Gombey, Moogahunya and child in their cone-shaped hut of saplings bound together with palm leaves and plastered with mud and dung.

The men still wore their traditional elongated bun hairdos bound up tightly in a cloth and a cloth wrapper covered their bottoms. Not much seemed changed over the centuries.

Despite its innate hardships the Himba have learned to survive very well in the arduous Kaokoveld and often move several times during the year to take advantage of prime grazing

Gombey, Gonyehah and Goryaha at work butchering a cow.
Note the traditional hairdos of the men which are adopted after marriage.

land for their cattle and their goats. They subsist largely on the milk of their animals. Their huts are small and simple, easily built cone-shaped structures.

   Arriving in the Kaoakoveld we stopped to visit with the first group of nomadic Himba we came across. Best to seize the occasion when we had it as who knew when we might come across a second group! They seemed as eager to see us as we were to see them and we promptly became friends. Their group, at least those who were visible to us, included three young families residing in their temporary cattle camp. They consisted of Chief Gombey and his first and second wives Moogahunya and Karentu. The other two couples were Gonyehah and Magaheyga and Gohreyah and Mautungwavee. If these weren't mouthfuls of names and syllables to learn and remember, I don't know what would be. They couldn't help their amusement with our struggles and were each so proud and pleased when we actually learned to pronounce them...and most amazing of all, remember them.

Moogahunya's daughter fixes her mother's hairdo.

Moogahhunya and her daughter make butter milk by shaking milk in the hanging gourds.

Once our new friends understood that we really were very eager to learn about their culture and traditions, and that we had crossed deserts and oceans to reach them, they invited us to stay with them for a few days. We couldn't have hoped for a better invitation. The only elements missing were their elders. As this was their cattle camp, only younger adults and children were present. Their elders, we were told, were comfortably ensconced at home base, which was somewhere under one very big and spreading African tree, two or three days walking distance away.

They were really terrific hosts and openly shared with us as much about their traditions as possible, like the different age sets and the ornate hairdos that represented each one. For example, until they are 10 years old, little girls wear two long and thick braids, almost like inverted cow horns, hanging down the sides of their faces. When they reach puberty the two braids are replaced by a series of tiny braids which fall all over their faces. After a rite of passage ceremony which celebrates puberty, all the braids are reassembled at the back of the head. This new coiffure indicates that they are now of marriageable age.

There are also hair rituals for the men who, at the time of marriage, cover their already long hair with a turban-like cloth, piling all their hair on top of and behind their heads. They often even augment the volume with small sticks before tying it up in the turban.

Married women are considerably more decked out than the men, which seems to be the norm in most cultures, tribal, western, eastern or otherwise. For the Himba women, their most important piece of jewelry is a special seashell necklace, which symbolizes fertility. These necklaces are very rare and are passed down from mother to daughter. Women also wear a large copper cuff and huge tubular copper necklaces. The Himba don't work with metal, so they must trade with other tribes to obtain these materials.

For Himba women the hairdo is of prime importance. It's not surprising that they share this fascination with hair creations with the Tuareg, Wodaabe and the Hamar. When you live in cultures which can provide little or no material anything for accessorizing the body and one's daily appearance, women will quickly make use of what's naturally theirs and " go to town" with their own hair. Long tresses are a symbol of beauty and very often a woman will make hers longer artificially by adding either hair from her brothers or vegetable fiber. This hairstyle is created on a woman's marriage day and is never altered afterwards. Included with the "do" is a tiny hat of goat skin, called "erembe," perched on the very top of her head, looking at times like rabbit ears. She simply moves this to the side if she needs to transport water or something else on her head.``

We were a total novelty to our hosts and they threw themselves into the joy of such an unusual encounter. So did we! They showed us how they lived, and more...we actually played "dress up." Moogahhunya thought that for us to truly understand them we should put ourselves in their clothes...similar perhaps to "putting oneself in someone else's shoes?" So, the women invited us to put on their animal skins and color our bodies with their special red hematite powder and animal fat confection. We readily accepted. Well...all but me. Somehow I knew instinctively that the red greasy powder would never come off either our skins or undergarments without submitting each to the equivalent of a minimum of five

Pine Sol-laced washings and rinsings on Super Load. Doubting that there was such a laundromat nearby that could handle all of us, I politely declined and gracefully opted to be the "dressor" rather than a "dressee." Once the make overs were complete, my now Himbatized ladies strutted around camp adjusting their newly acquired Himba tribal personas as they went. We were all hoping a neighboring Himba man might chance to stop by so we could see if he were duped. We were sure he would be.

When it was time to get ready for dinner, we all went down to the river and helped each other wash the red grease and powder off. Just as I suspected, it required double and triple soaping duty to get it out of our clothes. As for bodies, well, that was an even longer story. It really was a remarkable time, because how often do you get to be "Miss Himba for a Day" and dress up in her goat skins and body paint? What a treat and memory.

I won't say I wasn't a bit jealous. I would have loved a little Himba strutting myself. There's just nothing like putting on a well-used, molded-to your-body, complete with flounces, set of tribal skins; painting yourself with ochre from head to toe and feeling like you have truly tuned in to your deepest primal self. It's just that greasy stuff that throws me every time.

The next day we had more lessons in milking cows, and anything else Mougahhunyah or Gombey could think of, all transmitted to us through our Himba interpreters. It was Himba 101 on a three-day field trip!

We finally got to the point where we had questions that they could not answer because only the elders had been instructed in that more esoteric information. We had clearly graduated from Himba 101 and were now careening into Himba 202.

Young Himba girl wearing pre-puberty braids in her hair.

Chief Gombey suggested we go directly to their elders and talk with them personally. What an amazing new opportunity they were giving us. What an amazing time we had already had!!!

Chief Gombey told us where to find their families and we headed out the next morning. Several hours of bumping along what had once been a road built by the South African army

177

ten years before but hadn't been used since, finally led us to a huge tree in an open expanse, under which sat, as predicted, a group of about ten elders. The central figures were Geemooannee Muroungwa, chief of the Katchimba area, a man of about 60 but looking 80; and his younger brother Itha Muraingwa who looked about 65 but was probably 50. The sun can do that to you.

We introduced ourselves and were invited to sit down with them. For about an hour we asked a variety of questions about the Himba culture and traditions from birth and marriage customs to rituals of prayer and death. All our questions were answered without hesitation and in detail. They even included the animated visuals as the chief would send a little girl to get some important item and then he would ask an elderly woman, who might have been his own grandmother or mother, to demonstrate. We were enormously flattered that they should be so open with us.

When we finished our questions, we then asked, as we always do when lucky enough to have these encounters, if they had any questions they might like to ask us. The chief's younger brother said he had some. I was fully expecting some special ones about the odd behaviors and habits of white people, so his questions as he delivered them one by one were wonderfully surprising. We were mesmerized.

He began with, "Those men in the radio, are they in the radio or are they somewhere else?"

His next question: "Those airplanes in the sky…are there men in there and can they fly to God?"

His third question: "Every day a yellow ball comes up in the sky over here and goes down over there. Is it the same yellow ball every day or a different yellow ball?"

And his final question: "Why does it get dark when the yellow ball disappears?"

It's difficult to convey how privileged I and everyone with me felt to be present among these people at that moment. Their questions were certainly not due to any lack of intelligence, but to the grace to have survived all these centuries despite any intrusions from the modern world. Paul, our Namibian guide, did an excellent job of answering. The elders looked very satisfied.

We weren't the first whites to visit them. There were missionaries living less than a mile away who had lived among them for years. But I suspect that these Himba knew we were there to respect and honor their traditions, not change them. And so they in turn honored us by giving us a glimpse of a world that would have been otherwise impossible for us to know. What a gift!!

CHAPTER FIFTEEN

ON BECOMING A BUSH NURSE   "THE CONTRACT"

It was September, 1998 and I was once again in Niger for the Nomadic Festivals with a group of Turtle Travelers. We were now in Tuareg territory, having just spent a night camping on lovely dunes. We had eaten breakfast, the vehicles were all packed and we were heading out overland to our next destination. We didn't get very far because just beyond some nearby dunes was a small Tuareg encampment. I suggested that we stop and say good morning to everyone. It would be a great way to start the day.

We got out of the trucks and walked over to the tents, asking as we went if they minded if we paid them a visit. They seemed intensely happy to see us. The reason why quickly became evident. Lying on a mat on the sandy ground in one of the tents was a very sick little girl about 10 years old. As it was after the rainy season, everyone in the camp insisted that she had malaria. But the child was having respiratory trouble, and it looked more like pneumonia to me. As I always carry medicines, I had with me both malaria medicine and a very strong anti-biotic. I gave them both to the parents, and deferring to the opinions around me, I told them to put her on the malaria medicine immediately. Then, if by the time the sun went down, there were no change in her condition, they were to switch her to the antibiotic which would treat the pneumonia instead. We left, and I never knew if that child lived or died.

Typical Tuareg tents made out of goat skins. Air Mountains, northern Niger.
The same style tent can be found in the Timbuktu region of northern Mali, also a Saharan region.

Visitors are always welcome in the isolation of the desert.
Air Mountains, northern Niger.

The image of that child burned inside me for months, along with the pain and frustration of not having known how to interpret her symptoms in order not to waste valuable time. I decided that the solution would be to find a way to do an "internship" at a hospital in West Africa that treated cases similar to those I encountered regularly among my nomad friends. I tried first with Galmi Hospital in Niger. I wrote, armed with a letter of reference from my very wonderful doctor at home, Dr.William Devine, with whom I have discussed over the years all the illnesses I had seen in the bush and how best, given my limited lay experience and expertise, I might be able to help. Galmi turned me down, no doubt because of liability issues due to the more than glaring fact that I had no medical training whatsoever.

Tuareg tents are also made of reed mats, depending on the locale and the materials available for construction. Northern Mali, near the banks of the Niger River.

Setting up your tent is easiest when you have a few extra hands. Northern Mali near the banks of the Niger River.

My next step was to contact my close friend "Solo," Souleymane Coulibaly of TamTam Tours in Mali. Solo immediately provided the solution. One of his oldest friends was the Director of Medicine for the entire region of Mopti. Solo called Dr. Maiga who, once he understood that my intention was to help people in the bush who had no other recourse to medical help at all, invited me to come as soon as I wanted and he would arrange the time for me to spend learning alongside the appropriate doctors. There is actually a term in French for this kind of bush work I was hoping to do. It's called "secourist" and loosely translated, it means "first aid nurse."

In April, 1999 I flew to Mali and spent a week in Mopti working at both Somine Dolo Hospital and the Public Health Clinic. I got there a day early on Sunday so I had time to scope out the scene at the hospital before starting the first three days of my assignment Monday with Dr. Mariam Guindou, the pediatrician.

African hospitals can be enough to take your breath away. I remember the first time I visited one. We went into what I suppose could be considered an "outpatient treatment" room. There was a young girl about 10 years old lying on a cold white slab of a cracked tile counter, next to a big stained and cracked sink. She was getting an IV and needed some place to lie down. I guessed she had malaria. The white tiles of the counter did not look inordinately sanitary, nor did the hard porcelain of the countertop look inordinately comfortable. In fact, the entire hospital looked very dismal with its thoroughly faded and stained, institutional green painted walls throughout; patient rooms with plastic sheets rather inefficiently covering already very stained mattresses; and family members crouched on the dirty unswept floors beside each bed.

These hospital properties are generally enclosed by surrounding walls and there are lots of barren outdoor spaces where grass once grew but never will again. They were filled with people wandering around or sitting quietly, drinking tea, chatting with other family members and just basically trying not to worry. When the illness appears grave family members usually come prepared to stay for several days so they bring with them a collection of sleeping mats, teapots, cooking utensils and maybe a spare piece of extra clothing. These open air spaces were where the families lived until their relatives were ready to be discharged or died. Street food for purchase was always readily available outside the hospital gates which really was a blessing as the hospital did not serve food. Family and friends were expected to provide this on their own.

There was, however, another almost magical aspect of Somine Dolo hospital which was really an unexpected treat for the eyes and an experience in itself. Women who ordinarily wore their old and torn clothes, or remnants thereof, every day for doing all the daily labor of the household such as preparing meals, hauling firewood, watching small animals or children, or cleaning fish, took out their best clothes to go to the hospital, just as they would to a party.

The reason? First, there's the simple fact that women so often enjoy the chance to "gussy up." But there are other subtle social influences going on at the same time. Going to the hospital is something one only does when there is a serious health problem. Let's face it!

Malian women dressed in their very best outfits.

The average life span in Africa at its best is in the low 40's and the medical success rate for curing serious diseases probably isn't very high. But the dreaded hospital visit can magically transform itself into a spontaneous "social event" lifting each woman out of her worries and anxiety into a temporary preoccupation with looking beautiful. Nothing like a good dose of vanity driven adrenalin to help detour one's fears. Couple this with an innate societal understanding that people who are well dressed often get more attention and respect than poorer folk because they appear more prosperous than those who are poor...and you've got a great recipe for a constant flow of very well-dressed women and children. "

   And so, every day provided me with a glorious minute-by-minute West African Fashion Parade taking place right in front of me from morning 'til late afternoon, with all the models being neighbors. In the show were women decked out in an ongoing array of brilliantly colored African fabrics in all kinds of patterns and designs, lace trim on the necks and sleeves, multicolored flowing caftans topped with headscarves in matching or complementary colors. Little girls were dressed neatly in western style pinafores or party dresses with bows in their hair and little boys in spiffy shirts and pants made in China and all bought at the local market.

The unofficial "runway" for this exotic display began at the base of the old cracked cement block steps outside and led up into the main waiting area of the hospital. Upon arriving at the top of the steps each "local model" paused while she adjusted her clothing and proudly surveyed the room in front of her. She thinks, "Are any of my friends here? Does everyone see how beautifully my children and I are dressed? Is there anyone here who is better dressed than I am? Is someone wearing a new style I haven't seen yet? Perhaps a new fashion in from Ghana or the Ivory Coast?" Everyone was proud and worthy to be seen and I was certainly enjoying their brilliance.

Mopti's waterfront. Only a small section is visible as this is only one angle of a riverbank with curves.

The other very special ingredient of my "internship" at the Mopti hospital and Clinic was Mopti itself, Mali's second biggest city. It is still my favorite town in Africa. Referred to as the "Venice of Africa" it is the largest river port in Mali and sits at the confluence of the Niger and Bani Rivers. Its waterfront is a huge marketplace both impromtu and permanent at the same time. You can spot all the various ethnic groups of the river and the delta of Macina: Bambara and Songhai farmers, Bozo fishermen and boat builders, Sorkos and Somonos, Dogon from the Bandiagara Cliff, Peul and Touscouleur herders from the plains with their livestock.

Every afternoon after I finished my training at the hospital or clinic I would take a long stroll along the banks of the river back to my hotel, totally immersing myself in this colorful and animated atmosphere. Vendors spread their goods along the banks or carry them on their heads, local boats called "pirogues" ply the waters with their cargoes of people, animals and goods. Standing side-by-side, ankle to knee deep in the water, people do their daily bathing, laundry and dishes, or wash their cars, bicycles, goats and sheep. Everyone always seems happy. Nostalgically, I would often stop to visit with the Moors, who are Saharan people like the Tuareg but of Arab origin from Mauritania. They sell the big slabs of salt from the infamous Taoudeni mines far north of Timbuktu. The camel caravans that transport the salt from the mines to Timbuktu's river port don't stop in the town of Timbuktu. So you never get to see the huge, thick rectangular slabs into which the salt is cut for easy transportation south on the backs of camels. Most people have to be satisfied with seeing it for sale on Mopti's riverbanks after it has completed its river journey.

The next day I was very ready and eager to begin my three-day internship with Dr. Mariam. From 9AM to 4PM each day there was a steady stream of mothers and children.

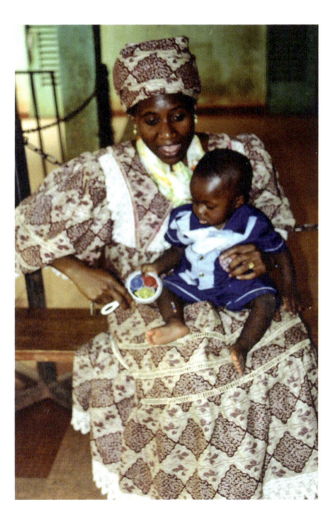

Dr Mariam Guindo, pediatrician with patient, sitting in the main reception area. of Somine Dolo Hospital, Mopti

Working alongside Mariam I observed closely as she questioned, examined, diagnosed and treated patients. And I took copious notes about everything. What I didn't understand I questioned and Mariam helped me. I remember the first time she told me to use my own stethoscope to listen to the child's difficult breathing. I was so nervous that I forgot to put the earpieces in to listen.

For the rest of the week I went over to the Public Health Clinic where I worked beside Dr. Sidibe Traore. The days were the same; from 9AM to 4PM we saw a non-stop stream of patients. Sidibe was equally patient, taking considerable time to explain things to me.

There was a lot of commonality in all the patients I saw, so it was fairly easy after a while to understand the symptoms and the diagnoses. Above all, I learned that the rule of thumb is to TREAT ALL THE SYMPTOMS AT ONCE. The reason is simple: even at the hospital in Mopti there is not the luxury to test whether the fever is due to malaria or pneumonia, or to which strain of each. Most tests are costly and have to be sent to the capital, Bamako, which also takes time. Most patients are simple farmers, herders or fisherfolk and they don't

185

have the money or the time to wait. Also due to costs, I learned another rule: that the drugs of choice are the most simple and generic. If the physician gets too specialized in his choice of drug, he runs the risk that the patient won't purchase the medicine as it is too expensive.

This "Treat for Everything at Once" system really works. Many times over the course of the week a mother would come in with a very sick baby. The diagnoses were made, the treatment prescribed and the mother told to come back in the next day or two for a follow-up. And when she came back, the child was invariably much better! This is exactly what I had needed to know eight months prior in that Tuareg tent with that very sick child: that I could have given that child both the malaria medicine and the pneumonia medicine to take at once, and it probably would have doubled the chances of her survival.

After my five days with patients I spent the weekend writing up all my notes, synthesizing what I had learned into my Bush Medicine Manual, which takes each illness, lists all possible symptoms, and appropriate medicines for each, with their dosages. I reviewed the entire text with Dr. Sidibe who gave me an A+, telling me I had learned in five days what they normally teach their aides over the course of a year. Doctor Devine back at home was equally impressed, assuring me that any intern or resident would give his or her right arm for the experience that I had had. I, of course, was still reveling in my remarkable good fortune!

Dr. Sidibe Traore, my teacher at the Public Health Clinic, Mopti

But...would it really work? The following September I headed off to Niger again for the Nomadic Festivals tours. Leslie Clark, who is my dear friend, fellow traveler and was an occasional Turtle guide, and I went a week early to visit our Wodaabe families before the Turtle Tours clients would arrive for the official trips. I had enough clients to send out two groups so I was leading the first group and Leslie would lead the second group a week later.

Leslie and I were both armed with a copy of Turtle's 35-page Bush Medicine Manual, as well as a quantity of the medicines I had identified in the Manual. We treated patients together during the first week while visiting our families so that I could "train" Leslie to use the manual. Then, when we split up to lead each of our Festivals Tour groups we treated separately. It was so rewarding to see "our patients" come back the next day to tell us how much better they were, especially the mothers who would bring back their now smiling babies to show us...no more ear infections, no more eye infections, no more coughs, no more diarrhea!!

In February, 2000 I went back to Mopti for a second week at the Hospital and the Clinic. As there was no official training program, I learned on the basis of the patients who appeared, so there was always something more to learn. This time my main teacher was Dr. "Fouss," Fousseyni Traore, who would eventually work with me as one of our Mobile Medical Clinic doctors.

From there I headed off to Timbuktu where I rendezvoused with my old Tuareg friend, Jiddou Ag Almoustapha, who had founded the association "Tinait"in 1998 to support the refugee Tuareg community who had just returned to Timbuktu. Jiddou and I had lost contact for about 10 years, due to a Tuareg rebellion and the insecurity it caused in the region from 1991 to 1996. The rebellion against the Malian government had been started by a dissatisfied faction of Tuareg in 1991 and had caused many non-political Tuareg to flee Mali overnight to the west into neighboring Mauritania. Everything they owned had to be left behind. Peace was negotiated in 1996 in a ceremony in which all the Tuareg rebels brought their weapons into Timbuktu and threw them into a huge bonfire called "La Flame de la Paix"the Flame of Peace. When the refugees returned to Mali in 1997 they found everything pillaged and their herds entirely lost.

By chance I ran into Jiddou in Timbuktu in 1999 and he told me about Tinait. I agreed to return to Timbuktu in February, 2000 after my second week of bush nurse training in Mopti, to see what I could learn and how I could help. Upon my arrival Jiddou and I immediately headed out to visit some of the refugees living in the bush. Armed with my Bush Medicine Manual, a big bag of medicines, my stethoscope and remembering to put it in my ears, I treated 40 patients the first day. The next day another 10.

This trip had a big bonus to it. Jiddou not only introduced me to the particular health needs of the nomad refugee communities of the Malian Sahara desert region, he also showed me their basic survival needs. They had many, including animal herd reconstitution, primary schools for their nomadic children, adult literacy programs, handicrafts co-ops, and water wells. TurtleWill had already begun humanitarian work of this nature in northern Niger with the Tuareg and Wodaabe nomads and so Jiddou's requests were right up my alley. Thus began a long partnership between TurtleWill and Tinait Association that would carry us through from 2000 to 2013.

Our February, 2000 medical foray visiting Tuareg inhabitants of the Sahara was also very interesting from a health point of view. Now I was seeing symptoms I hadn't seen in Mopti. So, once back in Timbuktu Jiddou and I went directly to the local hospital to meet with one of the doctors. Naturally he was quite affronted at first that a lay person like me should be running around in the bush treating people, but once I explained all: my training, my Bush Medicine Manual; as well as my limitations (for example, I don't give injections) combined with the fact that the people I help would have no other recourse to any form of medical aid, he became very willing to give me lots of additional information. I then sent the missing medicines back into the bush with Jiddou. The doctor even proposed to go into the bush with me on his days off to treat people, but unfortunately for a rather high fee! (It's no wonder the people in the bush need people like me.)

As a result of these two weeks of training in 1999 and 2000, plus my direct personal experience in Timbuktu, I did a test run of TurtleWill's Mobile Medical Clinics program in March, 2000 in Niger. Jan Toohey, Barbara Nolan and I arrived in Agadez, Niger on March 11 for the trial. Jan was our Resident Nurse; Barb, who had been an elementary school teacher, was our Education Consultant and Photographer and I was our "African Bush Nurse."

Jan had over 70 pounds of medicines which had been donated by friends in the medical community in her home town of Sun Valley, Idaho. We had everything from pediatric antibiotics to osteo-arthritis medicines, dermatological creams and shampoos, colorful soaps, endless bottles of aspirin, plus multivitamins and antacids from Barb, and malaria and iron tablets for pregnant or nursing mothers as well as for geriatrics.

We headed out the next day in our 4WD vehicle for a six hour drive to the camp of Chief

*Wodaabe Chief Tambari Girka and I
at Bundu Girka 1998*
**In Memoriam,
Tambari died in April, 2014**

Tambari Girka, a Wodaabe friend with whose family I had been visiting since 1997. The first three hours were on asphalt, followed by three hours through the bush across sandy track. Barb had just been with me in Niger the previous September for the Nomadic Festivals trip so she knew what to expect. Like so many other people Barb had fallen in love with the Wodaabe and was coming along just to repeat the experience. But Jan had done her first trip into Africa with me in Mali the previous November, through a far less desolate terrain and her eyes got wider as we pushed on deeper into the bush.

Barb was equally prepared for the wonderful welcome that awaited us when we arrived at the family well, "Bundu Girka." Every child and adult in camp came dashing over to greet us. We were so encircled with children's arms wrapped around our hips and hands entwined in ours that we could hardly stand up. Everyone was shouting the traditional greetings of "Foma, foma" (hello, hello) and excited "Mee Nanee Beldums" (I'm so happy!). Everyone remembered "Magana" (Barb) and all were very pleased that she had come back. They wanted to know where "Jumo," her husband Henry, was. As Wodaabe women are quite independent and usually leave home each dry season to go on "fombina," a two to three month foot journey south across West Africa selling their famous traditional herbal medicines and love potions, "Henry's at home" was an acceptable explanation. Clearly Magana was also out on fombina along with "Aissu" (me) and Jan.

Jan was in a state of semi-shock by this point. Even though Barb and I had "warned" her that the Wodaabe were the warmest and most wonderful people imaginable, I don't think we could have ever truly prepared her for such an all encompassing welcome. Chief Tambari promptly initiated her with her own Wodaabe name "Jumarey." We then made the rounds of all the family compounds to say hello to everyone, and introduce Jan, the newcomer. The children were all too excited to leave us alone with the adults so they streamed along with us. We set up camp nearby, and ate dinner underneath a million stars with Jan whispering "awesome" as she still looked around her in disbelief.

The next morning we devoted to our own orientation, setting up our little "clinic" in the only available shelter that no one else was using. It was made of straw and very crude but certainly "doable" for our first clinic. We had to wait to open the clinic officially until the following morning because this afternoon was reserved for a very important ceremony.

Jan holding Julbey's new baby at the Humto Ceremony held when the baby is eight days old. Julbey, as part of Wodaabe tradition, is not allowed to hold her baby until its eighth day. The baby's skin will eventually darken to be the same copper color as her mother Julbey in the photo.

Gajeri's and Julbey's first baby was now eight days old and according to Wodaabe tradition on this day the child would be named in the "Humto" ceremony. Quantities of calabashes filled with millet porridge had been prepared for all the guests. Julbey was sitting quietly on a mat, now actually permitted to hold her new baby for the first time since it was born, while all her friends and family came to greet her. Wodaabe babies when they are born are as pink as any Caucasian baby, and only eventually turn the deep copper color so particular to the Wodaabe. The baby's head had just been shaved according to Wodaabe tradition and the hairs had been dropped into a calabash of milk. They would then be taken out and made into a special amulet to protect the child.

Jan and I started the clinic the next morning armed with my Bush Medicine Manual. I began writing up cases but logging in people's names was a bit difficult. The Wodaabe live with a host of taboos; their name "Wodaabe" literally means "People of the Taboo." One of these taboos prohibits pronouncing your own name to someone else as well as prohibiting pronouncing the names of people who are close to you, especially your spouse or your first child. For this reason all Wodaabe have two names, the one that is unmentionable and the mentionable one. But even finding someone to mention the mentionable was a challenge.

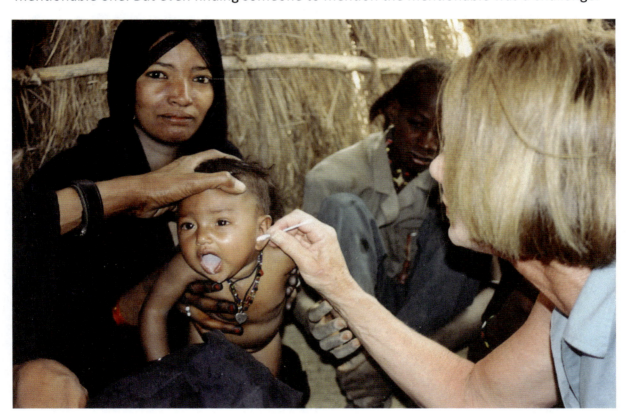

Jan treating Tuareg baby Hindou's ears at our first day's clinic.

There were at least 30 people waiting for us when we started. By 2pm we had treated about 40 people. We couldn't have arrived at a better time. A respiratory infection and conjunctivitis had hit everyone, especially the babies and the children. Even the Tuareg from neighboring camps had it. The pediatric antibiotics that Jan had brought were perfect, as were the adult medicines. We broke for lunch for an hour and treated until there was no more daylight.

We told all the mothers that they would have to bring their babies back each morning so we could continue to treat them. The second morning they were all back and smiling. Their babies had slept that night. They didn't wake up crying! Skin conditions on some were already clearing up. We had given multivitamins to people who had complained they had no appetite. Within hours they were hungry. We gave iron tablets to some very fatigued nursing mothers, and the next day they said they already felt stronger. Malaria medicines were already stopping fevers in some. Western medicines work so well here in these conditions because the body hasn't had a chance to build up resistances. We felt like we were really doing something!

Our Wodaabe friend and Clinic aide Suralji learning to mix the pediatric medicines
Girka Well, Maradi region, Niger.

Jan was totally in her element. She gave crying babies their medicines, held them and cuddled them, washed peoples' wounds, made sure everyone had extra soap to take home, even rubbed skin lotion into the legs of the older generation. She trained our Wodaabe aide Suralji, one of Chief Tambari's nephews, who had had a small amount of training elsewhere and wanted very much to help us with the clinic. He was totally dedicated and exactly the extra pair of hands we needed. Jan took him under her wing, teaching him to mix and dispense the pediatric medicines. By day three he was handling the repeat cases while Jan and I were handling the new ones.

On the afternoon of day five we closed the clinic. We had treated over 200 individuals in three days including mothers with babies. We had almost no medicine left and we needed to save some for the follow-up treatments for the children who had been told to come back for the next few days to be treated by Suralji. We decided to spend the rest of the day visiting all the special people we had come to know and love. We drove first to visit with the Tuareg mothers and babies at their nearby encampment. They had become like our second family in the neighborhood and it felt good to make a "house call."

"House Call"
The ladies of our nearby Tuareg family in their tent at Girka Well, Maradi Region, Niger.

Then, Jan went off to visit Suralji's mother again and rub more lotion into her legs. Barb and I went to visit Tambari's sons and their wives at their camp. The sun was setting and all the animals were lowing softly around us. It was one of those exquisitely peaceful and almost sublime moments. Everyone was stretched out on their mats and no one worried about looking good. It was all about relaxing and unwinding after a hard day's work.

That night back at camp we sat under the stars and reviewed our time together and among our Wodaabe and Tuareg friends. For Jan it was "the ultimate in humanitarianism." For Barb it was everything she remembered and more. For me, it was just perfect. I loved sharing again the joy of being with the Wodaabe with Barb, watching Jan so lovingly at work among these people we had come so far to see, and being able to help over 200 people in three days...at our very first Mobile Medical Clinic.

Suralji giving a pediatric antibiotic to a little Wodaabe boy at Tambari's camp.

On the morning of day six just as we were closing up our bags in our tents and preparing to leave I saw our Tuareg lady friends who lived nearby traipsing down the hill to us carrying their babies. "Oh no," I thought. "I hope nothing's wrong. They know they are supposed to go see Suralji at our little clinic shelter up there." Hima, my cook, was with them to translate. He explained that they had walked over from their own camp specifically to thank

193

us for all our good care and medicines that so helped their children. They wanted to make sure to see us before we left and were so glad to find us.

They had brought us gifts. Tahasamin and little Yasmin gave me one of their hand carved gourd bowls swinging in a cradle of macrame string. The Tuareg use it to keep food off the ground at night so the mice and kangaroo rats don't eat it. At my home in Arizona it still hangs outside my window, reserved for birds to make their nests in. It's now 14 years later and I have never forgotten its significance. Their words and gifts went right to my heart and were a perfect finale to our launch of the TurtleWill Mobile Clinics program.

We finished packing up, visiting everyone in Tambari's camp to say goodbye. Our final stop was at the rough shelter that had served as our little clinic. Just as expected, there was Suralji, surrounded once again by at least 20 mothers sitting patiently on the ground, waiting their turns for their children's medicines. He too was totally in his element and we knew he would continue where we left off. And so the TurtleWill Mobile Clinics program was "launched" in 2000 starting with this tiny shelter at Girka Well and 70 pounds of donated medicines from big hearted people in Sun Valley, Idaho.

In 2004, while working in Mali with the TurtleWill Mobile Clinics program, Dr Fouss, who had participated in my training in Mopti in 2000, and I gave my Bush Medicine Manual an overhaul, updating it to include the newer medicines and treatments that had been discovered in the previous four years. Although I did my training in French ,I had written my manual in English so that American medical volunteers could use it. It was determined so helpful by our Malian doctors and nurses, especially to all remotely situated medical staff that Fouss now translated it into French so we could distribute it to the various remote clinics we came across in Mali and Niger. It too took on a life of its own.

By 2008 the TurtleWill Mobile clinics were in full swing, operating in Niger, Mali and Ethiopia. By that point it had become a very extensive undertaking, traveling every three months in each country for 12 days including eight full days of clinics and with three Malian doctors and three Malian nurses, and medicines to treat a minimum of 2,000 to 2,500 people. Each clinic site within each of the three countries was visited every four months to maintain a continuity to the treatments.

One day that summer when I was at home in Arizona, my friend Rebecca came by for coffee. She looked around my museum-like home with all its artifacts from all over the world, told me that she often sees spirits and that she was seeing one now in my house. I asked her who it was and she said, "a child who followed you home from Africa." "Really?" I said. "Who is it?" Rebecca responded, "the child wants you to remember." "Well, can you at least tell me...is it a boy or girl?" Rebecca repeated, "As I said, the child wants you to figure it out for yourself." Rebecca and I had our coffee and a great-catch up but there were no more hints forthcoming about the child.

I pondered and pondered throughout the day and could not come up with any specific child that might have died recently. That night, however, I had a dream and in it was that same dying Tuareg child in the desert we had found lying on the ground in her family tent

Young Tuareg girl in typical dress of the Sahara desert of Niger.

This is what I imagine Fati would have grown up to look like if she hadn't died in 1998.

in 1998. In the dream she was now about 18 years old, She was sitting under a tree by herself and looked as though she had been waiting for me to arrive. As we drove up to her across the sand she got up and came over to greet me. I got out of the car and we took each others' hands. She told me her name was Fati.

"I want to thank you for honoring our contract," Fati said. "What contract is that?" I asked. She responded, "the one that we made together that early morning in the desert when I was dying...to find the means to heal as many people as we can....you've been fulfilling that contract ever since then with your Mobile Medical Clinics program! I am so proud of you."

It's true that the TurtleWill Mobile Medical Clinics flowed out of that unique encounter with an ease and a non-stop momentum. That we should come across a dying child so seemingly at random that early morning in 1998, in the middle of a desert tour, was a life-changing event for me. The overwhelming frustration of not being able to help her adequately led me to search hard and fast for a way to get myself trained to be a bush nurse so that I at least could be of some service in the bush.

The tiny makeshift Clinic at Bundu Girka was the beginning of a major TurtleWill program that grew exponentially yearly and operated in three countries: Niger, Mali and Ethiopia. By the time it ended in 2012 we had treated 102,000 patients. It was funded by both TurtleWill donors and by TurtleWill volunteers who paid to join the Medical Team for 15 days. It also created life-altering experiences for so many other individuals, both on the receiving end and the giving end!

So often I stop and wonder at the remarkably blessed life I have lived. I am instantly filled with gratitude for having been given the enormous gift of giving and healing, in which the TurtleWill Mobile Clinics played such a major part; for Guardian Angels showing up for me at just the right moments in the most unexpected places; for an amazing "Spiritual Contract" made between me and the unknown little girl dying in the sand.

And most of all, I am grateful for the privilege to live among peoples who, in addition to rigorously guaranteeing their own survival by a strict adherence to the rules of their cultures and traditions, follow their hearts in the most simple and innocent of ways.

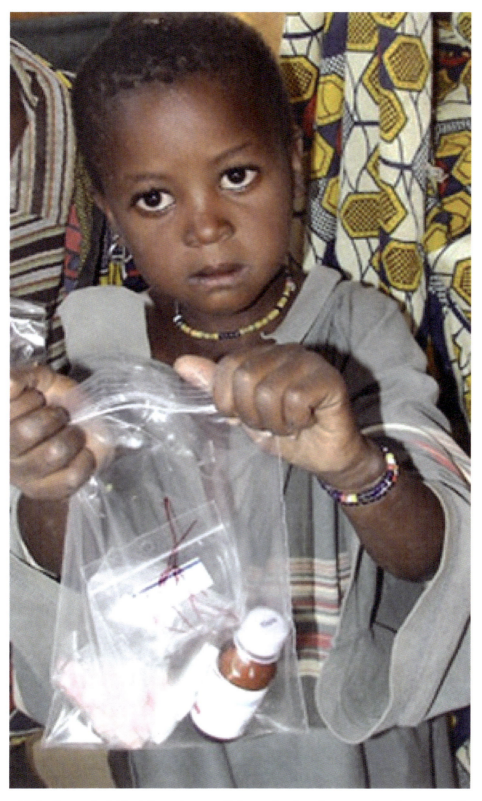

*Little Sonrai girl holding the medicines she has just received at one of
TurtleWill's Mobile Clinics, northern Mali.*

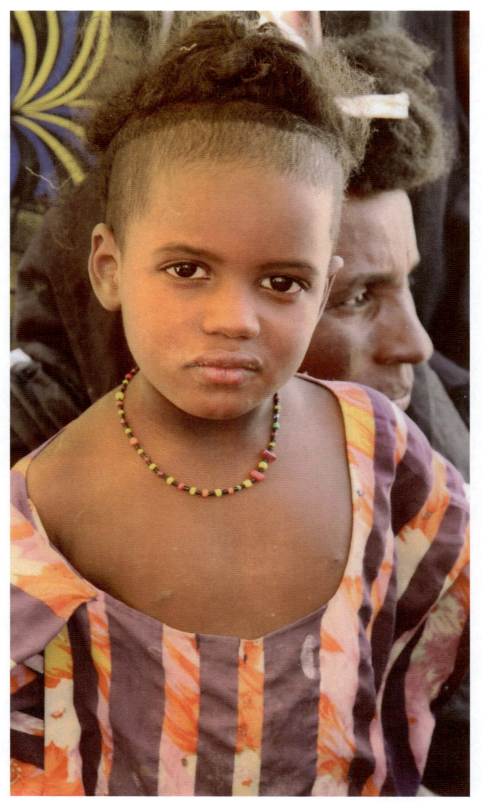

Little Wodaabe girl at one of our Mobile Clinics, Maradi region, northern Niger.

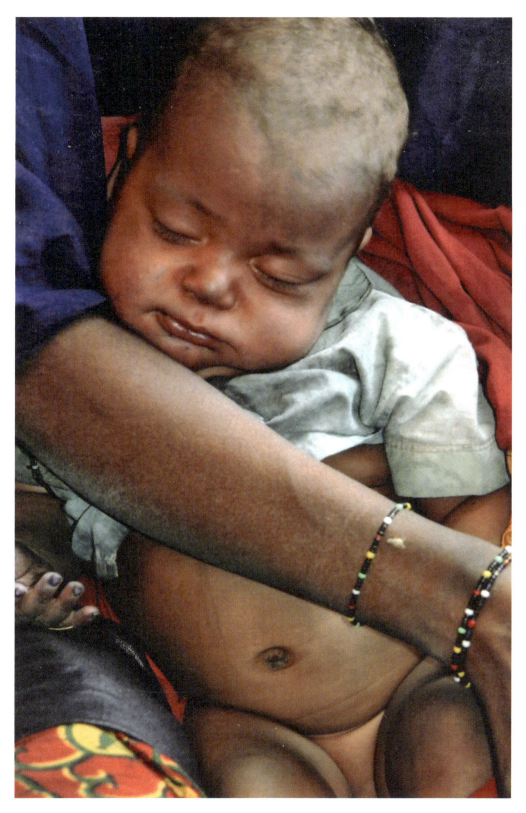

Babies can sleep anywhere, even in the middle of a TurtleWill Mobile Clinic.

Tuareg mother and son, TurtleWill Mobile Clinic, northern Niger.

Tuareg mother and son, Mobile Clinic, northern Niger.

TurtleWill's Nurse Ramatou with Mobile Clinic Patient, northern Niger.

Sonrai mother and son, northern Mali.

Fulani mother and child waiting to see pediatrician Dr. Mariam Guindo at Somine Dolo Hospital, Mopti, Mali.

*Last House Call with Mobile Clinic friend, Tahaseymin, Girka Well,
Maradi region, Niger*

MY THANKS ET MES REMERCIEMENTS

Working on the ground in Africa is not easy and requires, in some cases, the patience of saints.

This book of words and photos in honor of the persistent survival of these unique tribal peoples would not be complete without an expression of profound thanks and gratitude to my very special friends and colleagues, Africans and Europeans in the mix, who made Turtle Tours and TurtleWill both possible and successful.

Without them neither I nor all those individuals who have traveled with me would have had these rich experiences and encounters, nor the equally rich memories.
I also want to thank them each for the wonderful friendships we have shared over the years.

Irma Turtle "Aissu"

TO CHRISTIANE BLANC

Turtle Tours and TurtleWill could never have accomplished all that we did without you.
You were indispensable: a great Tour Manager, Expert Guide and a Wonderful Friend.
How synchronistic was our meeting up on the Ajjers Plateau in Algeria in 1985!
With enormous thanks to you and much love, Irma

Relaxing on the boat trip from Mopti to Timbuktu.

In her own traditional desert garb.

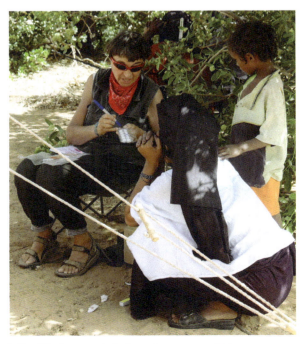

Christiane at one of our Mobile Clinics explaining dosages of the medicines prescribed for this mother and son.

In Niger

"Barney," Bernard Raymond Dunes Voyages, Agadez, Niger

My great thanks go to "Barney" as partner with Mano Dayak at Temet Voyages and then as

director of Dunes Voyages. As of 1989 Barney was responsible for all our in-country logistics including both Turtle Tours expeditions and TurtleWill humanitarian programs for the Tuareg and the Wodaabe. His amazing expertise, diligence and management skills enabled the successful achievement of all that we undertook. Our shared love for these peoples and our willingness to go many an extra mile for them made it very easy to work together.

Barney in his office in Agadez, overseeing in total detail all the logistics of Turtle Tours and TurtleWill's work in Niger.

Alhousseini Biki, Tuareg Educator, President IFI Association, Agadez

In 1999 TurtleWill began aiding Tamazalak School where Alhousseini was then Director. A remarkably compassionate and gentle man, he has always been available to listen to the needs and wishes of his people. He became equally invaluable to me as TurtleWill's In-Country Director for all our Tuareg projects. His dedication helped TurtleWill develop a massive humanitarian program for the Tuareg of Niger in which we funded Women's Micro-Credit Cooperatives, water wells, primary bush schools, middle school student residences and a 2004-2007 Mobile Medical Clinics program treating 21,000 patients.

Nassamou Malam, Woodaabe Tribal Chief. Bii Nga'en Lineage

I first met Nassamou in 1988 when he was a young nomadic cattle herder. He has consistently grown more involved with the general welfare of his people and is a co-founder of the Wodaabe organization BARAKA, focusing primarily on education for the people and veterinary help for the herds. As TurtleWill's In-Country Director of all Wodaabe projects, he helped to develop schools, wells, cooperatives and veterinary programs.
Today he is a tribal chief of the Bii Nga'en lineage of the Wodaabe tribe.

Alhousseini Biki, (on left) Tuareg Director of all TurtleWill Tuareg programs in Niger.

Chief Nassamou Malam, Wodaabe Director of all TurtleWill Wodaabe programs in Niger.
Air Mountains, 2008

Jiddou Ag Almoustapha in Timbuktu, 2008.

In Mali

Jiddou Ag Alnoustapha, Tuareg
President TINAIT Association, Timbuktu

I first met Jiddou in 1987 in Timbuktu when he was a young cameleer. A Tuareg rebellion from 1991 to 1996 in northern Mali forced many non political Tuareg to flee Mali overnight for refuge in Mauritania. When the rebellion ended and the refugees returned home in 1997 they found all their possessions and herds gone. In 1998 Jiddou founded Tinait Association to help reinstate all the returning Tuareg refugees. From 2000 to 2013 TurtleWill and Tinait worked together in the Timbuktu region aiding the Tuareg, Bela and Moor communities. Together we reconstructed lost herds, built five primary schools for remote villages including latrines, provided adult education classes, dug water wells, funded handicrafts cooperatives and provided treatment for 37,300 patients, all in the remote regions of Mali.

"Solo," Souleymane Coulibaly, Bambara, Director of Malian Tour Companies

I have known "Solo" since 1986 when we met on the banks of the Niger River in Mali. Through his adventure travel companies TamTam Tours and then Dougou Dougou Travel he has handled all the logistics of our Mali Overland adventure tours as well as our Malian Mobile Medical Clinics operating from 2005-2009. .Not only is he a highly professional business person, he is a great humanitarian.

Solo visiting me in Arizona in 1999. With him is my godson Daniel who spent 3 months working with Solo in Mali.
He told us it changed his life.
Also here is my assistant Jan.

Yohannes Assefa

In Ethiopia

Yohannes Assefa, Director, Red Jackal Tours, Addis Ababa

I have worked with Yohannes since 1990. Together we created a "perfect" itinerary to the various tribes in the Omo Valley as well as wonderful relationships with the tribal peoples themselves. We always had friends and "family" waiting for us at all destinations. Yohannes is a master of detail and a very caring tour guide. All my clients loved him. Yohannes also ran all the TurtleWill Mobile Medical Clinics in Ethiopia. I could count on him to handle all contingencies and details.

Tous Mes Remerciements et Gratitude

Je voudrais terminer mon petit livre de témoignage personnel aux tribus en exprimant aussi mes profonds remerciements et gratitude à mes chers collègues Français et Africains qui ont rendu Turtle Tours et TurtleWill possible d un grand succès. Tous sont devenus des amis du coeur.

AU NIGER.
Barney, Bernard Raymond.
 Mes grands remerciements vont à "Barney" comme partenaire avec Mano Dayak à Temet Voyages et ensuite comme directeur à Dunes Voyages. Barney était en charge de toute notre logistique y compris celle de Turtle Tours et des programmes humanitaires de TurtleWill pour les Touareg et les Wodaabe. Sa remarquable compétence, diligence et ses talents de gérance qui a permis le succès de toutes nos entreprises. Notre amour partagé pour ces populations tribales et notre volonté de faire un pas supplémentaire pour eux a rendu notre travail très agréable.

Alhousseini Biki , Tuareg Educateur , Préfet , Président IFI Association , Agadez.
 En 1999 TurtleWill a commencé à aider l école Tamazalak ou Alhousseni fut le directeur. Un home plein de compassion, chaleureux toujours disponible et à l écoute des besoins et des souhaits des gens. Il m'est devenu indispensable en tant que directeur intérieur pour TurtleWill prennant charge de tous les projets   des Touareg.. Son dévouement a permis à TurtleWill le développement humanitaire pour les Tuareg des coopératives micro crédit ,
 la construction des puits à l'eau , les écoles de brousse primaires , des résidences des l écoles moyennes et notre programme de cliniques mobiles de 2004 à 2007 qui ont traite 21,000 malades .

Nassamou Malam, Woodaabe Chef Tribal. Bingawa,
J ai rencontré Nassamou en 1988 quand il était un jeune pasteur nomade. Il a constamment évolué en prennant part aux besoins du bien être de son peuple, il est un des fondateur de
l' organisation BARAKA, en se consacrant à l éducation de son peuple et a l aide vétérinaire des troupeaux. Etant le directeur pour TurtleWill de tous les projets Woodaabe concernant des écoles, des puits, de coopératives, programmes vétérinaires.
il est aujourd'hui un chef tribal base a Foudouk.

AU MALI
Jiddou Ag Alnoustapha, Tuareg Président TINAIT Association, Timbuktu.
 J'ai rencontré Jiddou en 1987 à Tombouctou lorsqu' il était jeune chamelier. En 1998 il a fondé l Association Tinait pour aider à la réinsertion de tous les refugiés Touareg fuyant le Mali suite à la rébellion. Une fois la rébellion terminée et après le retour des réfugies chez eux en 1997, ils ont tout perdu, leurs   possessions et troupeaux. Avec l aide de TurtleWill, Jiddou était responsable de la reconstitution des cheptels, construction de 5 écoles primaires et de l éducation des adultes, des creusages de puits, des financements des co-ops
coopératives et   de superviser les programmes de cliniques mobiles de 2005 a 2009 ces cliniques mobiles on traité 37,300 malades dans des régions reculées du Mali.

"Solo," Souleymane Coulibaly, Bambara, Directeur de Compagnies de tourism Malian
Je connais "Solo" depuis 1986 lorsque je l ai rencontré sur les bords de la rivière Niger.
Il a pu a cause de son agence de voyage pour aventuriers TAMTAM tours et après Dougou Dougou Travel prendre charge de toutes les logistiques de nos "Malian Ciniques Mobile Médicales en brousse" de 2005 a 2009. Non seulement un grand professionnel en affaires,aussi un grand humanitarian.

My family at Dambaite, including the three little"Ilmas,"
proud new hosts of the
TurtleWill Mobile Medical Clinics in Hamar Territory.

Omo Valley, Southern Ethiopia.

About Irma Turtle and TurtleWill

   Irma Turtle is Founder and President of TurtleWill. Previously she was Director of Turtle Tours, an adventure travel company specializing in unique remote tribal peoples. In 1984, Irma left a lengthy career in advertising in New York and Brazil to seek something more personally meaningful. In 1985, after a trip to North Africa and a glimpse into the unique hearts, cultural traditions and ancient lifestyles of nomadic peoples, Irma launched Turtle Tours in tribute to the tenacity of these tribal groups to survive intact into the 21st century.

Irma at home in Cave Creek, Arizona, 2014.

   Irma's love for her tribal friends was reciprocated, giving her a personal entree into tribal societies. Through Irma's expeditions and tribal contacts she witnessed directly the many needs of these peoples who receive little or no help from their governments and she worked together with them to resolve their priorities. Recognizing that assimilation comes quickly when tribal people are forced to give up their traditions and way of life, her objectives were to keep these tribal communities and their lifestyles stable through education, healthcare and economic development. The result was the birth of TurtleWill in 1997. Her own tenacity plus the dedication of her many Turtle Tours travelers to her and her cause madeTurtleWill a success.

The name *TurtleWill* comes in response to the question *"Who will help these people?"* The answer: *"Turtle will!"*

   Working in Niger, Mali and Ethiopia TurtleWill's achievements included funding 35 remote primary bush schools for nomadic children; treating 102,000 nomadic patients through TurtleWill's Mobile Medical Clinics who would otherwise have little or no recourse for medical help; digging 56 clean water wells; funding 106 cooperatives that teach women skills, including micro-credit, foodstuffs, handicrafts and sewing. These cooperatives have empowered over 4,500 women to become respected income-earning providers got their own households and their communities.

In January, 2013 Irma closed TurtleWill, after passing the torch of its educational programs in Niger and Mali to three American foundations. Thus, Irma's TurtleWill legacy is carried on by *Caravan to Class* and *FACES* in Mali and *Rain for the Sahara and the Sahel* in Niger.

Irma is featured along with the Dalai Lama in an international television series, "Nomads of the Human Condition." Airing as of 2003 it focuses on each individual's humanitarian contributions. Irma was also featured on "Profiles in Caring"television show, about exceptional humanitarian projects around the world. Irma's segment aired as of March, 2008.

TO ALL THOSE PEOPLE OUT THERE:

THOSE WHOM I KNOW AND THOSE I DON'T KNOW

Thank you for taking the time to read my book!
Thank you for sharing my experiences with me.

I am both very honored and very grateful.

I hope I have brought you as much joy and pleasure in reading it
as the entire 30-year experience has brought me,
the journeys, the writing and the photography all included.

With best wishes to all

Irma Turtle   "Aissu"

Made in the USA
Lexington, KY
15 October 2014